Sports Law in the Czech Republic

Sports Law in the Czech Republic

Martin Procházka
Tomáš Capoušek

This book was originally published as a monograph in the International Encyclopaedia of Laws/Sports Law.

Founding Editor: Roger Blanpain
General Editor: Frank Hendrickx
Volume Editor: Michele Colucci

Wolters Kluwer

Published by:
Kluwer Law International B.V.
PO Box 316
2400 AH Alphen aan den Rijn
The Netherlands
E-mail: international-sales@wolterskluwer.com
Website: lrus.wolterskluwer.com

Sold and distributed in North, Central and South America by:
Wolters Kluwer Legal & Regulatory U.S.
7201 McKinney Circle
Frederick, MD 21704
United States of America
Email: customer.service@wolterskluwer.com

Sold and distributed in all other countries by:
Air Business Subscriptions
Rockwood House
Haywards Heath
West Sussex
RH16 3DH
United Kingdom
Email: international-customerservice@wolterskluwer.com

Printed on acid-free paper

ISBN 978-94-035-0314-1

e-Book: ISBN 978-94-035-0202-1
web-PDF: ISBN 978-94-035-0241-0

Printed in the United Kingdom.

The Authors

Martin Procházka graduated from the Law Faculty of the Charles University, Czech Republic in 2006. Following a few years in advocacy, he then went to work in football as the in-house lawyer of AC Sparta Praha from 2008 to 2014. He subsequently moved to the position of the Director of the Sports Department of the club from 2015 to 2017. He is also a member of the Arbitration Committee of the Czech Olympic Committee since 2012 and the Chairman of the Disciplinary Committee of the Prague Football Association since 2010. Between 2013 and 2017 he was also a member of the Legal Advisory Panel of the European Club Association. He has previously published *The Implementation of the FIFA Regulations on Intermediaries in Czech Republic (country report)* as a part of the publication *The FIFA Regulations on Working with Intermediaries. Its Implementation on National Level*, Michele Colucci (ed.), Sports Law and Policy Centre, 2015.

Tomáš Capoušek graduated from the Law Faculty of the Charles University in 1998 and subsequently earned a PhD from the Law Faculty of Charles University Prague and the MBA from the Czech University of Life Sciences Prague. Since 2002 he has been active as the attorney-at-law. He is also currently the member of the Disciplinary Committee of the League Football Association of the Czech Republic ('LFA') and the former member of the Appeal Committee of the Football Association of the Czech Republic ('FACR').

Table of Contents

List of Abbreviations

ADV CR	Anti-doping Committee of Czech Republic
CAS	Court of Arbitration for Sport
COV	Czech Olympic Committee
CSTV	Czechoslovak Union for Physical Education
CUS	Czech Union of Sport
ECA	European Club Association
EPFL	European Professional Football Leagues
FACR	Football Association of Czech Republic
FIA	International Automobile Federation (Federation Internationale de l'Automobile)
FIBA	International Basketball Federation (Federation Internationale de basket-ball amateur)
FIFA	International Federation of Association Football (Federation Internationale de Football Association)
FIFPro	International Federation of Professional Footballers (Fédération Internationale des Associations de Footballeurs Professionnels)
IBU	International Biathlon Union
IOC	International Olympic Committee
KSČ	Czechoslovak Communist Party
LFA	League Football Association
SPSS 2016–2025	State's Policy for the Support of Sport 2016–2025
SSA	Society of Sport Associations of Czech Republic
SVAZARM	Union for Cooperation with the Army
UCI	Union Cycliste Internationale
UCI ADR	Anti-doping Regulations of the Union Cycliste Internationale
UEFA	Union of European Football Associations
UNESCO	United Nations Educational, Scientific and Cultural Organization
WADA	World Anti-doping Agency
YMCA	Young Men's Christian Association

List of Abbreviations

General Introduction

Chapter 1. General Background

1. Following the change in the political regime in the Czech Republic in 1989 and the subsequent years of necessary deregulation of various areas of life formerly completely rigorously controlled by the state, the area of sport which during communism has been one of these many centralized ones, had gone through a turbulent period of destabilization trying to find the crucial balance between the necessary support and influence of the state and the equally necessary independence of the national sport associations, the Czech Olympic Committee and other important and often famous and historically influential sports organizations active in the territory of the Czech Republic.

§1. Historical Organizations

2. The historical development of sport in Czechoslovakia has been hugely influenced by the traditional non-governmental organizations active in the area of physical education, mainly by the Czechoslovak SOKOL organization (or 'Sokol'), established around 1862. Sokol, apart from being primarily the apolitical sports and gymnastic organization, gradually adopted concrete political and cultural views and promoted a complete specific way of life, trying to support the physical and moral growth of the Czech nation.[1] This organization also played a very important part in the development of the sports infrastructure in the territory of Czechoslovakia. The first Sokol gymnasium has been built in Prague in 1862 by Mr Vojtěch Ignác Ulllman, the renowned Czech architect influenced by the Viennese neo-renaissance style. The Sokol gymnasiums were built in a specific way, while having the place for workouts at its core, they also had additional infrastructure including a stage, a gallery and a special storeroom for the workout equipment. Following the first Sokol gym built in Prague, the local units of Sokol gradually built a huge number of Sokol gyms throughout the whole area of Czechoslovakia. In the modest economic circumstances of the second half of the nineteenth century these Sokol gyms functioned as important local centres

1. *See* the official website of Sokol - http://www.sokol.cu/.

for many sports, educational and cultural activities and hugely popularized the political and cultural views promoted by the Sokol organization.[2]

3. First Czech purely sports organizations were established around 1875 as rowing and skating clubs. It is estimated that around 1879 there was around forty-five clubs in the Czech territory engaged in sports and tourism. Among the most popular sports at that time were fencing, chess, rowing, skating and cycling.[3] Before the end of the nineteenth century sport started to slowly become part of the school education. This penetration of sport into school education was closely connected with the rise of the Olympic movement, as Mr Jiří Guth, a school teacher and a personal friend of baron Pierre de Coubertin was a member of the first International Olympic Committee established by baron de Coubertin in 1894. This led to his long endeavour to create the Czech Olympic Committee, which eventually succeeded in 1899, and the Czech Olympic Committee was again reinstated after the First World War in 1918, days after Czechoslovakia declared its independence.

4. Jiří Guth eventually became the general secretary of the International Olympic Committee in 1919 and the de facto right hand of baron de Coubertin. This led to the period of establishment, development and healthy activity of various private organizations concerned with sport and physical education in Czechoslovakia, YMCA and various academic societies being the key players among those.[4] This prolific era considered by many as the golden era of Czechoslovakia was eventually disrupted by the Second World War, interrupting the promising development of the young state in many areas.

§2. Sport During Communist Era

5. After the rise of communism in 1948, the Czech Communist Party (KSČ) started to strictly enforce the unification of the whole area of physical education, firmly opposing the idea of the federative organization of sport and physical education, which would have ensured the preservation of the former national sport organizations. The efforts aiming to preserve more democratic organization of the area of sport and physical education were eventually suppressed.[5] The tendencies towards unification led to the establishing of the Czechoslovak Union for Sport and Physical Education (ČSTV) in 1957, as the unified mass organization authorized to control and organize

2. *See* Ing. arch. Sedlecký, Jaroslav: Sokolovny a jejich odkaz současnosti (Sokol Gymnasiums and Their Heritage in the Present Day), časopis Stavebnictví 08/09, Informační centrum ČKAIT s.r.o., 2009.

3. *See* Kössl, Jiří, Krátký, František, Marek, Jaroslav: Dějiny tělesné výchovy II. (History of Physical Education II.), Olympia, Praha, 1986, pp. 73 et seq.

4. *See* Jakubcová, Kristina: Sport a olympijské hnutí v zemích Visegrádu, jejich vývoj a transformace v postkomunistické éře (Sport and Olympic Movement in the Visegrad Countries, It's Evolution and Tranformation in the Post-Communist Era), Univerzita Karlova v Praze, Nakladatelství Carolinum, 2012, pp. 87 et seq.

5. *See* Kössl, Jiří: Historie Českého olympijského výboru a olympijského hnutí, Obnovení Českého Olympijského výboru dne 21. 12. 1992 (The History of the Czech Olympic Movement, The Restoration of the Czech Olympic Committee on 21 12. 1992), ČOV, Praha, 1993, pp. 10 et seq.

the area of physical education completely.[6] The mass element was periodically promoted by the so-called Spartakiades, the mass gymnastic events, politically organized to celebrate the anniversary of the liberation of Czechoslovakia by the Russian 'Red Army' towards the end of Second World War in 1945.

6. SVAZARM (the Union for Cooperation with the Army), another of the Czechoslovak mass organizations in the area of sport and physical education, was established later in 1951 in the manner of similar organization in the Soviet Union.[7] Apart from the preparation of recruits for the basic military training, the training of military reserves of the army and organization of the preparation of the civilian defence, SVAZARM was in charge of the organization of sports and hobbies considered as related to defence activities of the state, among others motor sport, sport shooting, parachuting, scuba diving, aviation, etc. Certain activities were allowed to be pursued officially only within SVAZARM and therefore were under complete control of the communist regime. Even though SVAZARM allowed its members to pursue these specific activities, its members were concurrently obliged to actively participate in various events organized by the communist party. The Czech Communist Party itself governed the contents of the inner activities within SVAZARM and dictated and promoted the political ideology which was always linked with these activities. After SVAZARM was established, the existing local organizations pursuing the relevant activities were either integrated into SVAZARM or dissolved. Local associations and organizations which continued pursuing their activities were integrated into the so-called basic organization of SVAZARM controlled by district or municipal SVAZARM organizations, regional SVAZARM organizations and the central Committee of SVAZARM at the top of the whole structure. The activities within SVAZARM were financed by the state, through the Ministry of Finance and other cooperating bodies.

7. The existing national independent organizations were mostly dissolved and outlawed as they often promoted democratic ideas and values incompatible with the official communist ideology.[8] The assets belonging to these organizations were gradually transferred to Sokol and the Sokol organization was later overtaken by the ČSTV and the communist establishment. After this transformation the area of sport and physical education in Czechoslovakia has been regulated centrally by the state until the end of communism in 1989, with the last of the independent organizations officially dissolved in 1956. During this era the physical education in general was interweaved with the communist ideology, the successes of Czech athletes were often used as a propaganda by the communistic regime in its publicly proclaimed war against capitalism and the independence of the relevant organizations (for example the Czech Olympic Committee), common in any functioning democratic society, was only feigned for the sake of appearance.

6. *See* Act. No. 68/1956 Coll., on organization of physical education.
7. *See* Act. No. 92/1951 Coll., on military ability education and Act. No. 87/1952 Coll., on reorganization of military ability education.
8. *See* Act. No. 187/1949 Coll., on state care in the area of physical education and sport.

§3. Era of Deregulation

8. After the change of political regime in 1989 the tendencies towards decentralization and limitation of the state's influence in all areas of life within the society after years of strict regulation by the communist party were naturally high. The shape of the following years, however, was also highly affected by the process of separation of the Czech state and Slovak state, as the former Czechoslovakia formally ceased to exist on 31 December 1992.[9]

ČSTV and SVAZARM lost their dominant influence and the whole strictly centralized structure quickly eroded while certain new subjects were created and some of the existing organizations started to become independent in accordance with the newly declared Act No. 173/1990 Coll.,[10] which revoked the Act No. 68/1956 Coll., on organization of the physical education, and regulated certain relations concerning the existing sport organizations, mainly returned their historical property rights removed at the beginning of the communist era in Czechoslovakia.[11]

---

9. For more information on the separation of Czechoslovakia with emphasis on the sporting aspects see Jakubcová, Kristina: Sport a olympijské hnutí v zemích Visegrádu, jejich vývoj a transformace v postkomunistické éře (Sport and Olympic Movement in the Visegrad Countries, It's Evolution and Transformation in the Post-Communist Era), Univerzita Karlova v Praze, Nakladatelství Carolinum, 2012, pp. 114 et seq.
10. *See* Act. No. 173/1990 Coll., which revokes he Act. No. 68/1956 Coll., on organization of the physical education, and which regulates some further relations concerning the existing voluntary sport organizations.
11. *See* Act. No. 187/1949 Coll., on state care in the area of physical education and sport, Act. No. 71/1952 Coll., on organization of physical education and sport, and Act No. 68/1956 Coll., on organization of physical education.

Chapter 2. Sources of Sports Law

§1. The Deficient Legal Framework

9. There is no special legal framework regarding the sports law in the Czech Republic. Some lawyers may argue that sports law in the Czech Republic does exist, bearing in mind the broad definition of the term containing for example the regulations of the particular national sports associations (for example the Football Association of the Czech Republic and the Czech Ice Hockey Federation have a very thorough and with regard to their extent very extensive regulations governing their scope of authority) and similar regulations,[12] however, most legal authors would state that when compared to the more traditional legal disciplines (for example the civil law, the business law, the labour law), there is no sports law in the Czech Republic.[13] A certain compromise between these two positions can be found in the opinion that the sports law in the Czech Republic is evolving, trying to find its identity or status and does not yet have a precisely defined borderline.[14] Even the law faculties of universities in the Czech Republic, while being traditionally conservative about the classes they offer, have gradually added the sports law to their curriculums, mostly as an optional class for students who are interested in this particular area of law. All of this indicates that the sports law is on the upswing. At this point, however, we may describe the sports law in the Czech Republic with one of the biggest experts on legal aspects of sport in the Czech Republic, the Supreme Court Justice Michal Králík, as a cross-section discipline, joining together pieces from various areas of law with specific sporting aspects and principles.

10. As opposed to, for example, Slovakia, where the legal framework regarding sport is at the moment much more thorough and the former Slovakian Act No. 300/2008 Coll., on organization and support of sport (since 2008 covering areas of sport's organization not even specifically covered by the Czech laws in 2017), has already been replaced by the new and modern Act No. 440/2015 Coll., on sport, which has ambitions to provide the effective and modern mechanisms of management and

---

12. *See* Kubíček, Jiří: Sport a právo (Sport and Law), Masarykova univerzita, Brno, 2012.
13. The definition of sports law is divided. For the content definition of the concept see Králík, Michal: Právo ve sportu (Law in Sport), C.H. Beck, Praha, 2001. Also see Hamerník, Pavel: Sportovní právo s mezinárodním prvkem (Sports Law with International Element), Auditorium, Praha, 2007.
14. *See* Various Authors: Sportovní právo (Sports Law): Chapter 2 – 'On the Essence of Sports Law' by Hamerník, Pavel, Auditorium, Praha, 2012.

administration of sport,[15] the situation in the Czech Republic is legislatively much more deficient.

11. In the Czech Republic only the Act No. 115/2001 Coll., on support of sport, exists, containing only eight paragraphs and these mainly generally govern the tasks of the Ministry of Education, Youth and Sports and of the regional self-governing units (districts and municipalities), basic duties of the operator of sports facility and offences related to operating sports facilities. The act on support of sport is one of only two acts in the whole legal framework of the Czech Republic focused primarily on sport, the second being the Act No. 60/2000 Coll., on protection of Olympic symbolism, governing the rights and obligations connected with the use of the Olympic symbolism and the protection against its abuse which falls within the scope of authority of the Czech Olympic Committee.

12. However, even given the above-mentioned lack of special legal regulation of sport by the state, it cannot be said that there is a lack of regulation of sport in the Czech Republic. On the contrary, some of the national sports associations have extensive sets of rules governing and regulating various aspects of their sports. In this the influence and impact of the respective international associations is more than often the key factor. Thus for example the Football Association of Czech Republic has issued an extensive complex of rules regulating various aspects of football in the Czech Republic in compliance with the rules of UEFA and FIFA.

§2. The Sport Norms

13. Apart from the very scarce legal framework provided by the state, the sports environment as such is being governed by sport norms. The sport norms, as non-legal regulators of the athlete's behaviour in the certain area of sport, may be considered as comparable to the legal norms even though the sport norms miss certain very important attributes of the legal norms, enforceability by the state being the most important of them. The purpose of the existence of some sport norms may also be very distant from

15. *See* the explanatory memorandum to the Slovakian Act No. 440/2015 Coll., On Sport, which acknowledges the specificity of sport as a social phenomenon, performed by professional, amateur and non-organized athletes, with different status. Apart from athletes the Slovakian Act on sport defines various subjects in the area of sport – sporting experts, sport clubs, sport associations, national sport associations and national sport organizations and relationships between these subjects, therefore providing these subjects with legal status and proper institutionalization. The Slovakian Act On Sport also defines disputes in sport and the settlement of disputes in sports – (i) decisions made by sporting referees during the game, (ii) decisions made by the sport organization within its autonomy and (iii) decisions made within disciplinary proceedings. Several contractual types are defined in the relationships between athletes and sport organizations – (i) the professional sport's conduct contract, (ii) the amateur sport's conduct contract and (iii) the contract on preparation of the talented athlete. The Act On Sport also provides legal bases for the national sports representation and part of the Act is dedicated to the development of the Informational System of Slovakian Sport, the electronic evidence containing information regarding the subjects active in the area of sport in Slovakia and should ensure effective management and administration of sport (i.e. regarding the distribution of public funds and subsidies) on the national, regional and local level.

the purpose of legal norms, as certain norms regulating organization of sport competitions try to ensure a minimal degree of solidarity and equality between differently strong teams to preserve the uncertainty with regard to the sports result of the competition.[16] The sport norm in general typically determines the behaviour of the athlete, creates framework for such behaviour and usually determines the consequences of its breach. The existence of sport norms is a manifestation of the freedom of assembly and certain principles that are enshrined in the Charter of Fundamental Rights and Freedoms and in the Constitution of the Czech Republic,[17] which guarantees the right to peaceful assembly and the right of association. The sport norms may be classified[18] analogously to the legal norms as; (i) written sport norms and (ii) non-written sport norms.

14. The written sport norms are typically norms issued by the national sports association (i.e. the Football Association of Czech Republic in football, the Czech Ice Hockey Federation in ice hockey, the Czech Basketball Federation in basketball, etc.) to regulate the area of sport including the rules of the game, the relationship between stakeholders within the area of sport, transfer regulations, etc.). On the one hand, the written sport norms may be issued by the international sports organizations with worldwide scope or, on the other hand, by a lower segment in the organizational structure of the national sports association (i.e. regional or local sports association) with a very territorially limited scope. The national sports regulations are usually fundamentally influenced by the regulations issued by the international umbrella sports association (i.e. FIFA in football, IIHF in ice hockey, FIBA in basketball, etc.) or at least by the principles expressed within these international regulations while enabling certain local deviations. These national sports associations are associations according to the civil law and their inner norms and regulations are therefore the expression of the right of these associations to regulate their internal affairs based on their constitutional right of association founded on legal principle of separation of the state from the private associations and the legal principle of the right of the member of the association to protection against any decision of the association which is contradictory with the law or internal regulations of this association.[19] The state therefore does not approve the founding of private associations, only registers and keeps evidence of the existence of these associations and also does not interfere with internal affairs of these private associations as they have a right to self-government. These principles have been confirmed by the decisions of the Constitutional Court of Czech Republic.[20] We may consider the sport norms issued by the national sports association as the decisions of the bodies of private entities that bind all persons (natural and legal) who have voluntarily

16. *See* Hamerník, Pavel: Sportovní právo s mezinárodním prvkem (Sports Law with the International Element). Auditorium, Praha, 2007, pp. 24 et seq.
17. *See* Various Authors: Sportovní právo (Sports law): Chapter 3 – 'Sport Norms and Other Non-legal Sources of Rules of Athlete's Behaviors' by Sup, Martin, Auditorium, Praha, 2012.
18. For a specific classification of sport norms see Kubíček, Jiří: Sport a právo (Sport and Law), Masarykova universita, Brno, 2012, pp. 13 et seq.
19. *See* Hamerník, Pavel: Sportovní právo – Hledání rovnováhy mezi specifickou sportovní úpravou a platným právem (Sports Law: Finding the Balance Between the Specific Sports Regulation and Law and Positive Law). Ústav státu a práva AV ČR, Praha, 2012, pp. 14 et seq.
20. *See* the finding of the Constitutional Court of Czech Republic dated 12 Dec. 2006, reference no. I ÚS 90/06.

become members or contractual partners of these private entities.[21] Apart from the sport norms as decisions of the private entities, the other type of the written sports norm considered by the legal theory, are the written sport norms adopted in contractual form. In Czech Republic for example friendly tournaments and even long-term competitions of various types of football are popular, being played with different number of players (4+1, 5+1, 7+1) and with different rules of the game. These tournaments and competitions are not organized by the Football Association of Czech Republic and the rules of the game and other connected sports norms are created ad hoc for these tournaments. These sport norms do not have the character of the decisions of bodies of the private entities, but may be considered more as the contractual obligations, binding the participants who agreed to take part in these amateur sport events.

15. The theory divides the unwritten sport norms into two categories – sports customs and oral or implied arrangements of the participating athletes.[22] The typical sports custom which has no basis in the rules of the game is kicking the ball out of the pitch when the player of the opposing team is injured to interrupt the match and enable his medical treatment. These customs differ between various branches of sports and typically came into being by a long-term repetition. The typical example of the oral or implied arrangements of the participating athletes is the additional refreshment break agreed between both teams during a friendly match played during extremely hot weather. The unwritten sport norms may be considered as supplementary to the written sport norms in the situations where the written norms are a little vague or in situations not governed by the written sport norms at all.

---

21. *See* Various Authors: Sportovní právo (Sports Law): Chapter 3 – 'Sport Norms and Other Non-legal Sources of Rules of Athlete's Behaviors' by Sup, Martin, Auditorium, Praha, 2012, p. 43.
22. *See* Various Authors: Sportovní právo (Sports Law): Chapter 3 – 'Sport Norms and Other Non-legal Sources of Rules of Athlete's Behaviors' by Sup, Martin, Auditorium, Praha, 2012, pp. 45 et seq.

Chapter 3. Specificity of Sport

§1. Decreasing Trend in Public Financing of Sport

16. It is estimated that 50%–60% of the adult population in the Czech Republic is overweight. This puts the Czech Republic at the top of the unflattering list comparing the EU Member States. Apart from the traditionally unhealthy food regimen in the Czech Republic influenced by historical factors, one of the main reasons of this situation is the insufficient physical activity of the population in general and its continued decrease. To state the generally known facts – the physical activity is on the decline due to the trends of modern living and the nature of modern jobs, which are oriented towards sitting behind computers. However, the trend is exceptionally worrying with regard to children between 12 and 15 years of age, where approximately 25% of these children are overweight due to the family lifestyle where the parents simply do not lead and influence children towards sports neither by example nor by at least moral support. The lifestyle of children is therefore marked by spending time playing videogames or watching television while eating candy and drinking excessively sweet drinks and not being interested in any sport or physical activity at all. The obesity of the population leads to the increasing strain on state's budget in the area of health care. Given the above-mentioned tendency of the population to not participate in any physical activities, it seems even more important that according to the KPMG Report on drawing and use of funds for sport from lotteries in 2014, prepared for the Czech Olympic Committee, CZK 1.00 (one Czech crown) invested in the Czech Republic by the state into the support of sport brings a yearly saving in the amount of CZK 2.53 in the state's budget in the area of health care.[23]

17. In 2011 there have been 35,243 sports organizations (clubs, associations) registered in the Czech Republic with their main financial income coming from the households (mostly in the form of membership fees paid by members of these sports organizations) calculated at 42% of the total income.[24] This huge economical participation on sport puts financial strain on households and the rising expenses of households with regard to the financing of sport activities may lead to suppression of sport activities among the socially disadvantaged. Put simply, it is much cheaper to let the child sit at home and play videogames than to pay the membership fees and equipment necessary for the child to participate in sports. Most of the registered sports organizations have problems with operational financing. Between 2007 and 2011 the public funds allocated to sport stagnated with the extremely unfortunate trend of decreasing funds being

23. *See* the analysis on drawing and use of funds for sport from lotteries in 2014, April 2015, prepared for the Czech Olympic Committee, KMPG. The Analysis was made public on the website of the Czech Olympic Committee - https://www.olympic.cz/loterie/docs/posouzeni-kpmg.pdf.
24. The philosophy of financing of Sport in Czech Republic, Analytical – concept study, 13. 4. 2012, KMPG - http://www.olympic.cz/financovani/docs/koncepce_financovani_sportu_prezentace_v9a.pdf.

allocated to sport form the national budget of the Czech Republic. At that time (between 2007 and 2011) the local administrations and municipalities were the main provider of funding into sport while considering the funds provided from the public sector (by the state and by local administrations and municipalities) and there has been no complex interconnectedness between the funding from the local municipalities and from the state. With regard to the existing infrastructure, 91% of all the sport facilities in the Czech Republic were older than twenty years. The decreasing trend of the public financing of sport in the Czech Republic is obvious also according to the analysis of the financing of sport in in Czech Republic from 2009, which mentions that the public expenditure on sport per capita in the Czech Republic was the third lowest among all the EU countries. After calculating the public expenditure with regard to sport as the relevant percentage of the gross domestic product of the Czech Republic, this percentage was the fourth lowest among the EU countries (0.11% of the gross domestic product).[25]

§2. The Bankruptcy of SAZKA

18. The general crisis in financing of sport in the Czech Republic culminated and became publicly obvious in 2011, after the bankruptcy of the betting company SAZKA, owned at that time mostly by the national sport associations, which used the company's profits from betting and lotteries to finance their activities. SAZKA was historically established in 1956 under ČSTV as the only official bookmaker which enabled the bets on sport activities during the communist era in Czechoslovakia. In 1957 SAZKA started the immensely popular number lottery which is still under way.[26] Following the end of the communist era in Czechoslovakia in 1989, SAZKA was transformed into a company limited by shares and these shares came into the ownership of several national sport associations. Until the insolvency crisis in 2011 SAZKA has been a very important benefactor of sport, distributing hundreds of millions Czech crowns to national sports associations every year and the profits of SAZKA were one of the most important sources of financing of the Czech sport in general. The main reason of the insolvency crisis of SAZKA has been the building of the multifunctional stadium in Prague which served as one of the hosting stadiums for the 2004 IIHF (International Ice Hockey Federation) World Championship. During the insolvency several private investors tried to take control of SAZKA and following the conclusion of the insolvency proceedings the shares in the company eventually came into ownership of a private investor, which led to the complete ceasing of the financial contributions of SAZKA's profits to sport associations. This effectively meant that one of the most important financial flows into sport in the Czech Republic dried out without being replaced.

---

25. Analysis on financing of sport in Czech Republic dated 16. 4. 2009, prepared by Ministry of Education, Youth and Sport and Czech Olympic Committee and based on the 'Study of public and private financing of sport in Europe' organized and prepared by the French team during the French presidency of EU in 2008.
26. *See* the official website of SAZKA: www.sazka.cz.

§3. The State's Policy for the Support of Sport 2016–2025

19. The State's Policy for the Support of Sport 2016–2025 (SPSS 2016–2025) is a strategic document of the Ministry of Education, Youth and Sport approved by the Government of Czech Republic in 2016.[27] It follows the previous strategic documents prepared by the Ministry of Education, Youth and Sport – 'The State's policy for the support of sport (2011)', the 'Plan of support of the development of sport between the years 2015–2017' and also the document issued previously by the Ministry of Health – 'Health 2020' regarding the national strategy of the state in prevention of diseases and support of health in general. The purpose of these strategic documents is to establish priorities and long-term national goals within designated areas and to ascertain the key principles and strategies to support and implement by the state to eventually achieve these established goals.

20. The SPSS 2016–2025 acknowledges the above-mentioned tendency towards the decrease of healthy physical activity within the Czech population and establishes grounds to reversing this unfit trend by supporting the building of the sport infrastructure, to be used by the general public with the goal to provide the population (with the emphasis on the youth) with enough possibilities to incorporate physical activities into their everyday lives. The social aspect of sport and its role in preventing socially pathologic behaviours within the society is acknowledged at the beginning of the document and the sport's important role in maintaining the general health of the public is highlighted. Sport is considered a public service to be provided by regional administrations and municipalities and the state and to be further developed by clubs, associations, non-profit organizations, commercial subjects and the rest of the public.

21. The SPSS 2016–2025 establishes the following general priorities of the state concerning the area of sport in the Czech Republic:

- to stop the decrease of the physical abilities of children and youth;
- to stop the increase of obesity of children and youth;
- to increase the level of physical literacy;
- to decrease the economical participation of households and citizens in sport;
- to provide transparency, evidence and openness of information in sport;
- to support active struggle against negative elements in sport;
- to support equal opportunities;
- to support intra-departmental and intra-sectoral cooperation;
- to strengthen the cooperation of the state with the local administrations and municipalities;
- to involve sport experts and sportsmen in the decision-making processes of the local administrations and municipalities;
- to support the volunteering and coaching and similar leisure activities of adults.

22. The SPSS 2016–2025 has furthermore established strategic goals in various areas of development of sport in the Czech Republic.

27. The whole text of the State's Policy for the Support of Sport 2016-2025 is available on the official website of the Ministry of Education, Youth and Sport: http://www.msmt.cz/sport-1/koncepce-podpory-sportu-2016-2025.

Area 1 – The development of sport for everyone with the following strategic goals:

- to support the development of sport clubs and sport organizations which form the backbone of the system of organized sport in the Czech Republic; these sport clubs and sport organizations in ideal case should strive to prepare the attractive environment for sport to attract the general public to participate in various sporting activities;
- to strengthen the role of the regional and local sport centres; these sport centres could support the local sport clubs and sport organizations with its administrative apparatus and provide methodology and expertise, while also cooperating with the local administrations and municipalities to improve the decision-making in relevant areas connected with sport;
- to create suitable conditions for increasing number of people participating in organized sport, mainly increasing the number of members of sport clubs and sport organizations, thus emphasizing their social aspect;
- to support mass promotional and motivational events as instruments which could attract people who do not usually participate in sport activities;
- to create and to develop suitable conditions to emphasize the potential for social integration in sport;
- to use sport and physical activity as a means to develop and support the life in communities.

Area 2 – Supporting the growth of the membership base within amateur sport with the following strategic goals:

- to raise awareness of youth with regard to the various areas of sport;
- to support and develop the amateur sport of the youth regardless of the potential to become professionals or to represent the Czech Republic internationally with the main goal of preventing many children who failed to perform at the highest level from leaving their areas of sport completely and thus motivating them to stay active within their area of sport throughout their whole lives;
- to support and develop the amateur sport of adults.

Area 3 – The development of sport in schools and universities with the following strategic goals:

- to increase the number of classes which include physical and sport activities in schools and at universities and to support the development of school and university sport clubs, while bringing modern and attractive forms of sport to schools and universities;
- to innovate the system of school sport competitions while increasing the number of schools and students participating;
- to increase the number of free time sport activities available to students;
- to stabilize and to further develop the system of sport competitions at the universities to make it available to all students.

Area 4 – The expertise in the area of sport with the following strategic goals:

- to build the Sport Research Centre and to ensure that its findings and expertise will be applied in practice as the modern research and science is considered a weak area in the area of professional sport in the Czech Republic especially in comparison to other European countries;
- to innovate the system of education of experts in sport;
- to improve the quality of experts working with children especially between 5 and 10 years of age.

Area 5 – The reconstruction and building of sport infrastructure with the following strategic goals:

- to reconstruct and to develop the facilities of existing amateur sport clubs;
- to reconstruct and to develop the sport facilities of schools;
- to develop the sport facilities of universities;
- to build a strategic sport infrastructure for the national teams and regional training centres for talented youngsters;
- to modernize the equipment for the preparation of the national teams and talented youngsters.

Area 6 – The sport activities of the handicapped with the following strategic goals:

- to ensure the availability of sport for the handicapped;
- to create a comprehensive system of support for the talented handicapped youngsters and the national teams of the handicapped.

Area 7 – The competitive ability of national teams of Czech Republic with the following strategic goals:

- to ensure first-rate conditions for the preparation of the national teams of Czech Republic in the departmental sport centres established by the ministries;[28]
- to continue the programmes of support of the talented youngsters in cooperation with the national sport associations;
- to develop the connections between the system of education and the system of support and preparation of the talented youngsters to ensure the suitable sport development of talented youngsters during studies with emphasis on the middle school education and universities especially by creating specialized schools oriented at particular sports and sport disciplines to enable the symbiosis of studying and training;
- to support the successes of the national teams and representatives of the Czech Republic at international competitions in cooperation with the national sport associations;

---

28. These departmental sport centres are established by the Ministry of Education, Youth and Sport, Ministry of Interior and Ministry of Defence according to the Act No. 115/2001 Coll., on support of sport.

- to create the system of health care for the national teams and representatives of the Czech Republic and talented youngsters;
- to create the system of support for the retired members of the national teams and representatives of the Czech Republic;
- to further develop the professional organizations of coaches and trainers to improve the social status of coaches and trainers in the Czech Republic in general;
- to support the professional competitions and to improve the social status of professional athletes in the Czech Republic in general.

Area 8 – The commercial sport with the following strategic goals:

- to repeatedly organize and host important international and national sport events;
- to develop the services in the area of fitness.

23. The SPSS 2016-2025 directly acknowledges the necessity of a clear long-term state policy in the area of sport. This policy should have the three following pillars:

(1) Strengthening of the institutional support of sport in the area of both state support and the support provided by the local administrations and municipalities, while also clearly separating and subsequently coordinating the roles of both. To ensure the collection of data by independent organizations which should consequently provide valuable input into the decision-making in the area of the sport.
(2) General and apparent improvement of the legislation regarding the whole area of sport, enabling better implementation of the EU legislation and the decrease of the administrative and bureaucracy for sport clubs and sport organizations.
(3) The sport subsidies policy and the level of state support of sport should include the increase of funds to a level usual in the European Union, to ensure greater stability of funding of sport associations and to create control mechanisms of the effective use and spending of the subsidies provided by the state and the local administrations and municipalities.

24. The SPSS 2016-2025 predicts and expects the gradual increase of the total financial amount directed into the area of sport according to the flexibility of the national budget of the Czech Republic. Starting from 2018 a continual three-year financial plan should be prepared. The SPSS 2016-2025 anticipates future financing from the relevant chapter of the state's budget with both the investment and the non-investment part, the financing from the budgets of districts as a weaker connecting link and massive financing from the budgets of local administrations and municipalities with investments into the local sports infrastructure.

25. The monitoring of the implementation of the SPSS 2016-2025 will be carried out by the Ministry of Education, Youth and Sport itself. For the implementation of SPSS 2016-2025 the special expert working groups will be formed with the purpose of preparing two-year action plans of the implementation of the policy. Special interdepartmental working groups will be created to deal with issues touching the areas of several ministries and ensuring the inter-ministerial cooperation. As of 2017, the

Ministry of Education, Youth and Sport shall inform the Government of Czech Republic about the progress in the implementation of SPSS 2016-2025 once per every calendar year.

Part I. Organization of Sport

Chapter 1. Sports Governance

§1. Governmental Institutions and Bodies

I. The Ministries

26. The state support of sport in the Czech Republic is traditionally managed and directed by three of the ministries (the central bodies of the state governance) – the Ministry of Education, Youth and Sport, the Ministry of Defence and the Ministry of Interior. All three ministries apart from their internal organizational structure establish their own departmental sport centres to fulfil various tasks connected to the state's support in the area of sport. The ministries as central bodies of the state administration have been established by the Act No. 2/1969 Coll., on establishing of ministries and other central bodies of state governance, as amended, currently counting fourteen ministries governing selected areas of administration in the Czech Republic. The ministries are headed by ministers, who together with the deputy ministers and the prime minister form the Government of Czech Republic. The legal bases for the governance provided by the ministries may be found in the Constitution of the Czech Republic.[29]

II. The Ministry of Education, Youth and Sport

27. The Ministry of Education, Youth and Sport is the central body of state governance with regard to the preschool education, basic education, tertiary and further education, social programmes, research and development, international cooperation in the mentioned areas, academic degrees, youth care, physical education, sports, tourism and sports representation in the Czech Republic. Within the organizational

29. *See* Act No. 1/1993 Coll., the Constitution of Czech Republic. Mainly the Art. 2 of the Constitution of Czech Republic consisting of four paragraphs contains the constitutional basis for establishing the legislative, executive and judicial state bodies.

structure of the Ministry of Education, Youth and Sport the expert deputy[30] is in charge of the Section for Youth and Sport. The Section for Youth and Sport supervises the areas of sport, physical education and youth governed by the ministry and defines the fields of state's support to be provided with regard to sport, physical education and youth.[31] The Section for Youth and Sport fulfils tasks connected with the preparation and implementation of the strategic documents and official policy of the state in the designated areas, especially following the resolutions of the Government of Czech Republic. It ensures the fulfilling of obligations of the Czech Republic towards the European Union and the Council of Europe in the designated areas. The Section for Youth and Sport also carries out the founding competences with regard to the Anti-doping Committee of Czech Republic. Organizationally, the Section for Youth and Sport consists of two divisions – (i) the Division for Sport and (ii) the Division for Youth.

28. The Division for Sport performs task and fulfils obligations arising for the state mainly from the Act No. 115/2001 Coll., on support of sport, and from the international conventions and resolutions of the Government of Czech Republic in the area of the state's support of sport, tourism, sports representation of the state and other similar areas. The Division for Sport also inspects the management of public funds granted to subjects in its field of activity. The Division for Sport is organizationally structured into the following departments with their own tasks and agenda:

- the Department for the financial support of sport;
- the Department for the policy in the area of sport;
- the Department for the investments and infrastructure in the area of sport;
- the Department for cooperation in the area of sport.

29. The Division for Youth is responsible for the state's care in the area of youth and children. This includes mainly certain areas of the formal and informal education of the youth, the education of the social and youth workers and preparation of the strategic documents regarding the State's Policy towards the youth. The Division of Youth is organizationally structured into the following departments:

- the Department for the financial support of sport;
- the Department for the formal and informal education.

---

30. The Act No. 234/2014 Coll., on the state's service, as amended, defines the positions of the expert deputies in charge of the sections of the ministries as opposed to the political deputies appointed by the members of the Government; every member of the Government appoints maximum two political deputies.
31. The Organizational Regulations of the Ministry of Education, Youth and Sport with its amendments (the description of the activities of the departments of the ministry, the organization established by the ministry) and the Organizational Structure of the Ministry of the Education, Youth and Sport are both available at the official website of the Ministry of Education, Youth and Sport: www.msmt.cz. The Organization Regulations of the Ministry of Education, Youth and Sport is a normative internal regulation issued in accordance with the Act No. 2/1969 Coll., on establishing of ministries and other central bodies of state governance, which regulates the scope of authority of the organizational sections of the ministry.

III. The Department Sport Centres

30. The Act No. 115/2001 Coll., on support of sport, describes the role of the Ministry of Education, Youth and Sport with regard to the department sport centres in its paragraph 3 in the following way – apart from establishing its own department sport centre the ministry also coordinates the activities of the department sport centres established by the Ministry of Interior and Ministry of Defence. Currently three department sport centres established by three different ministries operate in the territory of the Czech Republic:

(1) the University Sport Centre established by the Ministry of Education, Youth and Sport;
(2) the Army Sport Centre DUKLA established by the Ministry of Defence;
(3) the OLYMP Sport Centre established by the Ministry of Interior.

The department sport centres are mostly concerned with creating suitable conditions for the athletes representing the Czech Republic at international level – the world and European championships, the Olympic Games and other significant international championships – in particular and traditionally mostly individual sports. All three department sport centres support in total by estimate 1,000 athletes every year, one-third of this number in the junior category.

IV. The University Sport Centre

31. Apart from the Anti-doping Committee of Czech Republic, which will be described in a subsequent special chapter of this monograph, the Ministry of Education, Youth and Sport has established the University Sport Centre as the organizational unit of the state. The University Sport Centre has been established on 1 March 2003 as the educational expert department with the purpose of creating material, social and technical conditions for athletes representing the Czech Republic at the highest level in particular areas of sport. The support provided by the University Sport Centre is organizationally structured into ten sport sections – athletics, judo, speed canoeing, slalom canoeing, swimming, fencing, ice skating, tennis, sport games – basketball, handball and volleyball, academic representation.[32] The organizational structure of the centre is structured into four departments – the sports and technical department, the economic and personal department, the organizational and administrative department and the department of sport sections. The University Sport Centre is being managed by the director, directly appointed by the Minister of Education, Youth and Sport. The centre is financed from the state budget through the chapter belonging to the Ministry of Education, Youth and Sport and most of its financing is used for creating material conditions for athletes in its various sport sections. The top athletes representing the Czech Republic internationally selected above all according to their sport performance are in the employer/employee relationship with the centre, predominantly being employed as

32. For more information about the sports the University Sport Centre supports and the University Sports Centre in general see the official website of the University Sport Centre: www.vsc.cz.

sport instructors. The University Sport Centre does not operate any sport facilities entrusted by the state, it rents all the facilities it uses for the preparation of athletes.

V. The Army Sports Centre DUKLA

32. Another important part of the state sport support is ensured through the Army Sports Centre DUKLA established in its current form by the Ministry of Defence.[33] Its predecessor, the Army Sporting Club, was founded in 1948 to support the development of sport within the army. The former military sports unit now functions as a modern sport club, which supports athletes in various sport sections – athletics, cycling, canoe, rowing, modern pentathlon, canoe slalom, shooting, skiing, parachuting and the section of various sports (supporting also athletes from very diverse areas of sport as karate, beach volleyball, swimming, freestyle motocross, kickboxing, bobsleigh, etc.). The main task of the Army Sports Centre DUKLA is to secure the national and resort (i.e. army international competitions) sport representation of the Czech Republic and to prepare a junior team of athletes, while in cooperation with connected sport organization helping with the preparation of children and youth. The Army Sports Centre DUKLA is financed from the state budget through the chapters belonging to the Ministry of Education, Youth and Sport and the Ministry of Defence. The Army Sports Centre DUKLA is allowed to manage and operate the sports facilities entrusted to the Ministry of Defence by the state. The centre supports its athletes by offering them employment contracts. The most successful of the athletes employed by the centre (usually after reaching a medal at widely recognized international event such as European championship or World Championship) are offered a chance to become professional soldiers and to receive additional payments and better conditions.[34]

VI. The OLYMP Sports Centre

33. The third department sport centre has been established by the Ministry of Interior in 2009 and officially renamed OLYMP Sports Centre at Ministry of Interior in 2016. Its main purpose is to prepare top-level athletes for the representation of the Czech Republic in the following areas of sport – athletics, boxing, cycling, motorsport, swimming, pellet shooting, rifle shooting, tennis, triathlon, volleyball, weightlifting, biathlon and assorted sports.[35] The assorted sport sections have been divided into summer sports department and winter sports department, with winter sports covering cross-country skiing, alpine skiing, speed skating, bobsleigh and ski jumping. The summer sports department covers badminton, speed canoeing, yachting, sport gymnastics, rowing, taekwondo and trampolining. The OLYMP Sports Centre supports its member

33. *See* the official website of the Army Centre DUKLA: www.duklasport.cz.
34. The number of professional soldiers recruited from athletes cooperating with the Army Centre DUKLA keeps changing, but in 2016 roughly thirty athletes participated in the special military training in the military academy in Vyškov.
35. For more information see the official website of the OLYMP Sports Centre: www.olympcsvm.cz.

athletes (officially employed by the Ministry of Interior) by providing a regular monthly wage based on the long-term performance of the athlete and also by financial contributions which help the member athletes to cover the costs of their training. The OLYMP Sports Centre also provides training, rehabilitation and regeneration infrastructure and facilities and necessary coaching and medical personnel. The cooperating athletes are divided into two categories – sport instructors and contractual athletes. The sport instructors, usually the top athletes in the Czech Republic, receive full wage and financial contribution to cover their training costs. The contractual athletes, usually young perspective athletes not yet at their peak performance, do not receive any wage, but usually receive a financial contribution which at least partly covers their daily costs (food, nutritional supplements, equipment, etc.) and a financial contribution to cover their training costs. The particular amounts of these contributions are based on the performance of the athlete and are reset before every season. The OLYMP Sports Centre is financed from the state budget through the chapters belonging to the Ministry of Education, Youth and Sport and the Ministry of Interior. The OLYMP Sports Centre is allowed to manage and operate the sports facilities entrusted to it by the state.

VII. The National Council for Sport

34. The National Council for Sport is the advisory body of the minister in charge of the Ministry of Education, Youth and Sport. The minister chairs the meetings of the National Council for Sport. The mission of the council is to suggest the concrete solutions of actual problems in the area of sport.[36] The declarations of the council have advisory character. Every member of the council is responsible for a specific area of expertise and provides incentives regarding this area to the council. Every member of the council is also entitled to establish working groups of experts in the area of sport concerned with issues in his area of responsibility. Apart from the experts in various areas of sport, the National Council for Sport is constituted of the representatives of the regions (association of districts, Federation of cities and municipalities, association of local administrations). As of 2017 the National Council for Sports has thirty members.

§2. The Czech Olympic Committee

I. The History of the Czech Olympic Committee

35. The Czech Olympic Committee (COV) was established on 18 May 1899. Its history is rich and at times very poetic as its establishing is connected with the person of the Czech middle school teacher Mr Jiří Stanislav Guth-Jarkovský (1861–1943), one of the twelve founding members of the International Olympic Committee established in 1894, who participated at the first modern Olympic Games in Athens in 1896 as the only Czech participant and returned home very enthusiastic about the Olympic idea. After his return from Athens, Mr Guth-Jarkovský, who was not an active

36. *See* the official website of the Ministry of Education, Youth and Sport – www.msmt.cz.

sportsman himself, became one of the most famous officials and propagators of Czech sport. At the end of the nineteenth century the territory of the current Czech Republic was part of the Austrian Hungarian Empire and under a very strong Austrian influence. After his return from the first modern Olympic Games in 1896, Mr Jarkovský, who was a close personal friend of baron Pierre de Coubertin, the founder of the International Olympic Committee and a father of the modern Olympic Games, started to propagate the Olympic idea in the Czech and the German magazines with the goal to prepare the environment for establishing the Czech Olympic Committee. After initial difficulties the Czech Olympic Committee was established in 1899 and immediately started working on ensuring and preparing the participation of Czech athletes at the 1900 Olympic Games in Paris. This endeavour turned out to be successful, following the work of the Committee in total five Czech athletes participated at the 1900 Olympic Games in Paris and Mr František Janda Suk won the silver Olympic medal in the discus throw.

36. Even though at that point the sovereign Czech state did not exist, the Czech Olympic Committee acted autonomously until 1914. After the First World War, when Czechoslovakia declared its independence in 1918, the COV was re-established as the Czechoslovak Olympic Committee. Mr Guth-Jarkovský served as the Director of COV for the first thirty years of its existence between 1899 and 1929. Between 1919 and 1923 he also served as the general secretary of the International Olympic Committee and within the international Olympic movement was well respected, which initially led to the VIII. International Olympic Congress being summoned to Prague in 1925. This prestigious Congress, held under the patronage of the first president of Czechoslovakia, Mr Tomáš Garrigue Masaryk, made several organizational decisions regarding the form of the Olympic Games. Some of these decisions remain relevant even in the present day, most important of these probably being the authorizing of the autonomy of the Winter Olympic Games.

37. During the time period between the world wars the COV gradually established itself as the important part of the sporting landscape of the newly born state. While being partly financially supported by the state, one of its most pressing and important tasks was finding financial sources to cover its operational costs. In 1933 new statutes of the Czechoslovak Olympic Committee were adopted, giving the COV more precise form and competence.[37] Following that, COV started establishing technical committees led by experts in various areas. The COV often cooperated with then supreme sports body of the state – the Czechoslovak All-sporting Committee, established in 1928, and in cooperation with this body created the institution of the so-called Olympic Supervisors, scouts who kept overseeing the training of the athletes and sport clubs and determined the selection of athletes for national representation teams by preparing expert assessments of their preparation and performance.

38. After the Second World War and the change of political landscape the communist regime used the performances of Czech and Slovak athletes and sport in general as propaganda to strengthen its position. Even though physical education and

37. *See* Kolář, František: 'Vývoj olympijského hnutí v Česku' ('The Development of the Olympic Movement in Czech Republic'), the article is available on the official website of the Czech Olympic Committee (www.olympic.cz), http://www.olympic.cz/docs/osmus/vyvoj_olympijskeho_hnuti_v_cesku.pdf.

sport itself were supported by the state, until 1989 the Czechoslovak Olympic Committee was strongly influenced and directed by the communist party and its functioning during that era cannot be considered compatible with functioning of a sports body within a democratic society, i.e. the refusal of the Eastern Bloc countries including Czechoslovakia to participate at the Olympic Games in Los Angeles in 1984. The Czechoslovak Olympic Committee as an independent organization has been established after long years on 25 April 1990 and registered by the Ministry of Interior generally as a special organization representing the Czechoslovak interests within the international non-governmental organization (in this case the International Olympic Committee). The former seven times Olympic winner, the famous Czech gymnast Věra Čáslavská, has been elected the director of the newly independent COV, which functioned until the separation of the Czech and Slovak state in 1993.

39. Following the end of Czechoslovakia and the separation of the Czech and Slovak state in 1993, the former Czechoslovak Olympic Committee (COV) was also separated with two national (Czech and Slovak) Olympic committees as successor organizations. The statutes of the newly established Czech Olympic Committee were approved in January 1993 at the founding Plenary Session of the Czech Olympic Committee (COV) and the former Director of the Czechoslovak Olympic Committee Mrs Věra Čáslavská[38] was elected as the new Director of the newly established Czech Olympic Committee.[39]

40. The newly approved statutes stated that the COV unifies national sport associations, federations, sport organizations, unions, the segments of the COV, citizens of the Czech Republic and corporate bodies supporting the Olympic movement. The statutes also defined the sources of financing of the COV as subsidies from the state, donations, contributions from the IOC and Olympic Solidarity, and donations from natural, legal persons and sports associations. Other sources of financing stem from the educational, sports, cultural and economic activities of the COV. The COV also participates on the financial profit from selling commemorative coins and medals issued in connection with organizing the Olympic Games. One of the important financial sources was also the income from the lotteries and betting connected with the Olympic Games. The new COV has been temporarily acknowledged by the Executive Board of the International Olympic Committee on 16 March 1993 and finally fully acknowledged at the IOC's Plenary Session on 23 September 1993.[40]

---

38. *See* the introductory speech of Věra Čáslavská at the founding plenary meeting of the Czech Olympic Committee held on 21 Dec. 1992 at Kössl, Jiří: Historie Českého olympijského výboru a olympijského hnutí, Obnovení Českého Olympijského výboru dne 21. 12. 1992 (The History of the Czech Olympic Movement, the Restoration of the Czech Olympic Committee on 21 Dec. 1992), ČOV, Praha, 1993, pp. 19 et seq.
39. *See* Jakubcová, Kristina: Sport a olympijské hnutí v zemích Visegrádu, jejich vývoj a transformace v postkomunistické éře (Sport and Olympic Movement in the Visegrad Countries, It's Evolution and Tranformation in the Post-Communist Era), Univerzita Karlova v Praze, Nakladatelství Carolinum, 2014, p. 143.
40. For more information about the history of the Olympic movement in the territory of the current Czech Republic see the official website of the Czech Olympic Committee: www.olympic.cz.

II. The Current Czech Olympic Committee

41. Due to the historical political and legislative changes in Czechoslovakia and later also due to the separation of Czech and Slovak Republic, the basic documents and the structure of bodies of the Czechoslovak and later Czech Olympic Committee have changed many times. The current COV is an association in conformity with the Act No. 89/2012 Coll., the Civil Code, and according to its current statutes acknowledges its successorship after the original Czech Olympic Committee founded originally by Mr Jiří Guth-Jarkovský in 1899. This continuity has been acknowledged immediately after the restoration of the Czech Olympic Committee in December 1992.[41] The main activity of the COV according to its statutes is the development and propagation of the Olympic ideals, and thus contributing to the physical and spiritual education of citizens of the Czech Republic and especially youth in the spirit of Olympism. As a reaction to historical events the statutes emphasize the autonomy of the COV and its resistance against any type of pressure, e.g. political, legal, religious, or economical, which would prevent the COV from abiding by the Olympic Charter.[42] The statutes acknowledge that beside its main activity, the COV may perform secondary activities, mainly economical, to supplement its main activity or to better administer its property. These secondary activities could particularly be the providing of various services in the area of regeneration or recondition, leasing objects owned by the COV, lending the Olympic symbolism to products contributing to the development of the Olympic movement according to the rules of using the Olympic symbolism in compliance with the Olympic Charter and any other conduct of business according to the laws of the Czech Republic which is not in breach of the Olympic Charter.

III. Membership within the Czech Olympic Committee

42. Both legal and natural persons may be associated within the COV. The natural persons need to be fully legally competent and without a criminal record, while fully acknowledging the Olympic Charter and the Statutes of the COV. The following rules regarding the membership in the COV apply:

- any member of the IOC who is simultaneously the citizen of the Czech Republic is automatically the member of the COV;
- the national sport associations with membership within the international sport associations and federations governing Olympic sports are automatically members

41. *See* Kössl, Jiří: Historie Českého olympijského výboru a olympijského hnutí, Obnovení Českého Olympijského výboru dne 21. 12. 1992 (The History of the Czech Olympic Movement, the Restoration of the Czech Olympic Committee on 21 Dec. 1992), ČOV, Praha, 1993, pp. 31 et seq. (the programme of the Czech Olympic Committee approved by the Executive Committee of the Czech Olympic Committee on 16 Mar. 1993).
42. *See* the statutes of the Czech Olympic Committee ratified by the Plenary Session on 11. 4. 2013, amended on 24. 4. 2017, p. 2, available on the official website of the Czech Olympic Committee (www.olympic.cz), http://www.olympic.cz/upload/files/Stanovy-COV-24-4-2017.pdf.

of the COV, for each sport only one national sport association may be a member of the COV;
- the national sport associations with memberships within the international sport associations and federations acknowledged by the IOC and governing non-Olympic sports are automatically members of the COV, for each sport only one national sport association may be a member of the COV;
- the organizational units of the state and other organizations governing the areas of physical education and sport are members of the COV;
- the representatives of the structural units of the COV are also members of the COV;
- honorary members and personas who have provided great services to the idea of Olympism are also members of the COV;
- the representatives of the Committee of athletes who participated at the Olympic Games are members of the COV.

The Plenary Session of the COV decides who will be accepted as a new member of the COV, usually after the applicant passes the trial period up to four years long. The trial period may be shortened or even removed by the decision of the Plenary Session of COV following the proposal of the Executive Committee of COV.

IV. The Internal Structure of the Czech Olympic Committee

43. The structural units of the COV whose representatives are members of the COV are the Czech Olympic Academy, The Czech Olympians Club, the Czech Fair Play Club, the Czech Sports Associations, the Organizations and Institutions Club and the Czech Paralympic Club.

The Czech Olympic Academy is a scientific, informational and promotional centre of the Olympic movement in the Czech Republic established in 1987 following the request of the IOC towards its members to establish national Olympic academies with the purpose of continuous studying of various aspects of the Olympic movement, especially its philosophy and history and transferring these Olympic ideas into everyday life. The Czech Olympic Academy cooperates with various scientific and pedagogical institutions and through its trainer/coach section endeavours to develop suitable conditions for the activities of the Professional Trainers Union based at the COV.[43] The Czech Olympic Academy has two main bodies, the Council with seventeen members being the main one and the Presidium of the Council with three members

43. According to its Internal Regulation published at the official website of the Czech Olympic Committee (www.olympic.cz), the Professional Trainers Union has been established as the trainers section within the organizational structure of the Czech Olympic Committee. This makes the Professional Trainers Union a specific part of the organizational structure of the Czech Olympic Committee, but not the structural unit according to the statutes of COV. The Professional Trainers Union provides its members mainly with legislative, legal, health and educational support while also trying to improve the social status of professional trainers and coaches in Czech Republic.

(the chairman and two vice-chairmen) being the executive one. The activities of the Czech Olympic Academy are financed from the budget of the COV.[44]

The Czech Olympians Club is the successor of the Czechoslovak Olympians Club established in 1975. It unites the former Czech Olympians and supports the ones who face social, health and other problems.[45] Anyone (athletes, trainers and substitutes) who have in their life participated at the Olympic Games, may apply for membership at the Czech Olympians Club, which functions mostly as the platform where the former participants of the Olympic Games meet. The Czech Olympians Club has two main bodies, the board with fifteen members being the executive one and the General Assembly being the main one.

The Czech Fair Play Club traces and rewards acts of fair play while granting three different types of awards – the main fair play award, the diploma and the letter of thanks. The Czech Fair Play Club rewards the important and long-term promotion of fair play, exceptional acts, long-time educational activities concerning the youth or successful sport representation of the Czech Republic connected with promoting the idea of fair play throughout the career.[46]

The Czech Sports Associations, Organizations and Institutions Club represents the non-Olympic national sports associations and various other organizations and institutions active within the area of sport in the Czech Republic within the COV, where it protects the interests of the non-Olympic sports and supports the cooperation between the Olympic and non-Olympic sports.[47]

The Arbitration Committee of the Czech Olympic Committee has seven members elected by the Plenary Session of COV. The Arbitration Committee primarily functions as the supreme appeal body regarding disputes concerning the breach of anti-doping rules in the Czech Republic, in case of decisions made by the bodies of the members of the COV, or in case of disputes connected with the Olympic Games. It may also serve as the supreme appeal body in other disputes concerning national sport associations in case the statutes of these national sports association establish its competence. The

44. *See* the current valid and effective Statute of the Czech Olympic Academy approved by the Executive Committee of the Czech Olympic Committee on 20 Mar. 2013 on the official website of the Czech Olympic Committee: (www.olympic.cz), http://www.olympic.cz/docs/cov/coa_statut.pdf.
45. *See* the current valid and effective Statute of the Czech Olympians Club approved by the General Assembly of the Czech Olympians Club on 14 Nov. 2008 on the official website of the Czech Olympic Committee: (www.olympic.cz), http://www.olympic.cz/upload/files/CKO-status.pdf.
46. *See* the current valid and effective Statute of the Czech Fair Play Club approved by the Executive Committee of the Czech Olympic Committee on 26 Nov. 2014 on the official website of the Czech Olympic Committee: (www.olympic.cz), http://www.olympic.cz/upload/files/novy-status-CKFP.pdf.
47. *See* the current valid and effective Statute of the Czech Sports Associations, Organizations and Institutions Club approved by the Executive Committee of the Czech Olympic Committee on 6 No. 2017 on the official website of the Czech Olympic Committee: (www.olympic.cz), http://www.olympic.cz/upload/files/Statut-CKSOI.pdf.

Arbitration Committee of COV may also serve as the first instance body in case its competence is established by a valid arbitral clause.[48]

44. As far as the organizational structure goes, the COV has the following bodies – the Plenary Session of COV, the Executive Committee of COV, The Chairman of COV and the Vice-Chairmen of COV, The Auditing Committee of COV, The Arbitration Committee of COV, the Ombudsman of COV.

While the Plenary Session is the supreme body of the COV meeting at least once per calendar year and comprising of representatives of the national sports associations, representatives of the Committee of athletes who participated at the Olympic Games, the Czech member of the IOC and the representatives of the structural units of COV, the Executive Committee is the executive body with the maximum of twenty-five members including the Chairman of COV and five vice-chairmen. Of these five vice-chairmen, one is elected the first vice-chairman and one is elected the Vice-Chairman for non-Olympic sports (elected by the Czech Sports Associations, Organizations and Institutions Club as opposed to all the other vice-chairmen elected by the Plenary Session of COV). The Auditing Committee consist of three members elected by the Plenary Session and its main task is to audit and inspect the processes and economic activities of the Executive Committee of COV and the secretariat of the COV. The Ombudsman of COV is elected by the Plenary Session according to the proposal of the members of COV and his task is mainly the protection of rights granted to the members of COV by the Olympic Charter, the Statutes of COV and other democratic principles.

V. The Activities of the Czech Olympic Committee

45. The Statutes of the COV define the property and economic activities of the COV in its Article XV. According to this article the sources of property of the COV are particularly the following:

- the donations and contributions from IOC and the Olympic Solidarity;
- the donations and contributions from natural and legal persons and sports organizations;
- the incomes from educational, sports, cultural and economic activity of the COV;
- the subsidies from the public sources;
- various incomes from other sources.

The last category refers to incomes arising from activities described in the Article II Section 3 of the Statutes of the COV, which enables the COV to perform any profitable activity according to the Czech law as long as the activity is not in contradiction with the Olympic Charter. The Article XVI of the Statutes of the COV describes the official symbols of the COV and states that the COV is entitled to create its own business logo

48. *See* the current valid and effective Statute of the Arbitration Committee of the Czech Olympic Committee approved by the Executive Committee of the Czech Olympic Committee on 6 Nov. 2013 on the official website of the Czech Olympic Committee: www.olympic.cz, http://www.olympic.cz/upload/files/7f1o3xflcg-STATUT-Rozhodci-komise-2013.pdf.

to be used in the marketing activities of the COV. The official logo, the official flag and the official anthem of the COV are subject to approval of IOC. As defined in the final provisions of the statutes, the Statutes of the COV have to be in compliance with the Olympic Charter at all times. In case of any contradiction between the statutes and the Olympic Charter, the Olympic Charter shall prevail.

§3. The Umbrella Sports Associations in the Czech Republic

I. The Czech Union of Sports

46. The Czech Union of Sports (CUS) was established in 2013 by the transformation of the former CSTV.[49] The CUS unifies the national sports associations in the Czech Republic, the sports clubs and other sports organizations established according to the Czech Civil Code. According to its statutes the CUS is self-governmental and voluntary alliance of legally, organizationally and financially independent legal persons. The main activity of the CUS is the organization of sports activities for its own members and the general public and other activities connected to sport in general. Natural persons may become members of the CUS through their membership in the legal persons associated in the CUS. The CUS itself is the association according to the Czech Civil Code. The main task of the CUS is the creation of optimal conditions for sports activities organized by its member entities – the sport clubs, the sport organizations and the national sports associations. The CUS also provides various additional services to its member entities within the area of sport in the Czech Republic and also helps to provide and ensure the financing of the sport activities organized by its member entities. Through its membership in the Czech Olympic Committee the CUS represents the interests of its member entities within the COV.

47. According to the Statutes of the CUS,[50] within its main activity the CUS especially performs the following activities:

- within its member entities organizes sport activities for its members and the general public and provides education in the area of sport;
- strives for creating ideal material, legal, organizational and other conditions for supporting and development of the area of sport and its member entities;
- cooperates with the public authorities, local administrations and municipalities in the Czech Republic;
- cooperates with various sports organizations in the Czech Republic and worldwide;
- administers its own property and legal rights;
- helps to organize programmes for development of sport, the education of experts in the area of sport, and organizes various sport and cultural event independently;

49. *See* Ročenka ČUS 2016 (The Yearbook of CUS for 2016), edited by Opatrný, David, Nakladatelství Olympia, Praha, 2017, pp. 4 et seq.

50. *See* the current valid and effective Statutes of the Czech Union of Sports approved by the Plenary Session of the Czech Union of Sports on 23 Apr. 2016 on the official website of the Czech Union of Sports (www.cuscz.cz), http://www.cuscz.cz/files/1799ZDQ.pdf.

– according to its possibilities provides various other services for its member entities.

To support its main activities mentioned above the CUS may also in conformity with its statutes perform the following additional profitable and business activities:

- providing of services within the areas of sport and education;
- hospitality and restaurant services;
- massage and regeneration services;
- accountant and tax services;
- plumbing and similar services;
- selling of liquors and alcoholic drinks.

To supplement and improve its main activity the CUS may also create business corporations or acquire shares in such business corporations and establish and run educational, pedagogic and schooling institutions in all legal forms.

48. The Statutes of the CUS recognize two types of membership with different rights and duties of the members – the basic membership and the special membership.

The basic membership is relevant for: (i) the sport clubs and sporting unions as the entities organizing the sport activities and connected activities in their local areas and for (ii) the national sports associations as the entities with the nationwide authority which direct, manage and organize the whole particular disciplines and areas of sport and which are exclusively responsible for the preparation and organization of the representation of the Czech Republic at the international level in these particular sport disciplines.[51]

The special membership is relevant for: (i) the district organizations of the CUS with local authority and for (ii) the natural persons. These entities may become the members of the CUS after submitting a written application including the relevant excerpt from the register of associations and the copy of their statutes, which have to be compatible with the Statutes of the CUS. The sport clubs and sporting unions become members of the CUS after becoming members of the respective district organization of the CUS with local authority and they exercise their membership rights and fulfil their membership duties through these district organizations of the CUS. The national sports associations with nationwide authority and the district organizations of the CUS with local authority become members after the approval of their application by the Plenary Session of CUS. The natural persons become members of the CUS through their membership in the particular sport club or sporting union at the moment these entities become members of the CUS through the above described process. The CUS administers the list of its own members. The extent of the membership rights and duties of the CUS members is determined by the type of their membership.

The membership rights belonging to all members (both basic and special) are the following:

51. According to the official website of the Czech Union of Sports (www.csucz.cz), there are currently seventy four national sports associations with nationwide authority with membership within the Czech Union of Sports.

- the right to participate in the sporting events organized by the CUS according to the level of performance and the expertise of the member;
- the right to use the facilities of the CUS according to the fixed terms and conditions;
- the right to use the services provided by the CUS according to the fixed terms and conditions;
- the right to terminate the membership in the CUS at any moment.

The membership rights belonging to basic members of the CUS are the following:

- the right to delegate their representatives to the Plenary Session of CUS (the sport clubs and sporting unions exercise this right through the district organization of the CUS they belong to);
- to provide the organs and bodies of the CUS with suggestions, propositions and incentives.

The membership duties common for all members of the CUS are the following:

- to abide by the statutes and regulations of the CUS and the resolutions and decisions of the organs and bodies of the CUS;
- to perform the sports activities in the spirit of fair play and the Olympic ideas.

The membership duties connected with the basic membership of the CUS are the following:

- to pay the membership fees properly and on time;
- to administer the proper evidence of their members (natural persons);
- to provide the organs and bodies of the CUS with truthful and relevant data regarding its organizational and economic situation to ensure the just distribution of funding within the CUS.

The membership in the CUS may be terminated the following ways:

- By a written notice of the member entity about its withdrawal from the CUS delivered to the CUS. The decision of the withdrawal has to be taken by the competent body of the said member entity according to its statutes and the member entity is obliged to settle its obligations with the CUS before the end of the calendar year during which is the membership of this entity terminated.
- By deleting of the basic member of the CUS who has not paid its membership fee after a formal notice with a subsequent time limit for payment of the membership fee out of the list of members.
- By a legal termination of a membership entity of the CUS, this entity is obliged to settle its obligations with the CUS before its termination.
- By an exclusion of a member by the decision of the Plenary Session of CUS based on a suggestion of the Executive Committee of CUS for a serious breach of the Statutes of the CUS or of the decisions of the organs and bodies of the CUS, or for a conduct incompatible with the membership within the CUS; the

district organization of the CUS with local authority may be excluded for improper management of the CUS matters in the region.
- The membership of a sport club in the CUS is terminated through the termination of its membership in the district organization of the CUS.
- The membership of a natural person in the CUS is terminated through the termination of his/her membership in the member entity of the CUS or through the termination of the membership of this member entity in the CUS.

The decision of termination of the membership of the member of the CUS may be appealed by the affected member to the Revision Committee of CUS within fifteen days after it is delivered to this member. While considering the appeal the Revision Committee of CUS decides whether the membership of the member has been terminated according to the Statutes of CUS and the laws of Czech Republic and either confirms or revokes the decision.

49. The Czech Union of Sports has the following bodies and organs:

- the Plenary Session of CUS as the supreme body;
- the Council of CUS as the statutory body;
- the Executive Committee of CUS as the executive body;
- the Revision Committee of CUS as the controlling body.

The Plenary Session of CUS is the supreme body of CUS and is composed of the delegates of the membership national sports associations and the delegates of the membership sports clubs and sporting unions. The Plenary Session meets at least once a year upon being summoned by the Executive Committee of CUS at least thirty days before its meeting. For the Plenary Session to be able to make decisions the overall majority of all delegates has to be present. The following matters have to be decided (or in case of budgets approved) by at least three-fifths of the present delegates:

- the determination of criterions for the use of the financial sources of the CUS and the allocation of these sources;
- the budget of the costs of the CUS used to satisfy the needs of the member entities of the CUS;
- the budget of the Executive Committee of CUS including the budget of the Revision Committee of CUS;
- the transfer of property owned by the CUS (real estates, property shares, etc.);
- the changes in the Statutes of the CUS;
- the changes in the Statute of the Revision Committee of CUS;
- the granting and revocation of the title 'the honorary Director of CUS';
- the decision on termination of the CUS and the liquidation of its property.

The following matters may be decided by the simple majority of the present delegates of the Plenary Session of CUS:

- The approval of the results of fulfilling of the budgets of the Executive Committee of CUS including the budget of the Revision Committee of CUS and other approved budgets.
- The approval of the report on the activity of the Executive Committee of CUS.
- The approval of the report on the activity of the Revision Committee of CUS.
- The determination of the prospective programmes of activities of the CUS.
- The establishing and termination of the subsidiary society of the CUS.
- The approval of the rules of procedure and the rules of election, the election and the removal of the Director of CUS and the members of its Executive Committee of CUS and the election and removal of the members of the Revision Committee of CUS.
- The changes in implementing the regulations to statutes of CUS.
- Any other decision of the Plenary Sessions of CUS.

The bodies elected by the Plenary Session of CUS and its members have four-year long terms of office. In case of death or resignation of a member, the next Plenary Session elects his subsidiary for the remaining term of the office. The Plenary Session also decides by the simple majority of the present delegates whether the Chairman of the Executive Committee or the Members of the Executive Committee may carry out their terms of office as the employees of the CUS or whether the nature of the working relationship between CUS and the Chairman of the Executive Committee and the Members of the Executive Committee during their terms will be different.

50. The Executive Committee of CUS is the executive body of the CUS and it fulfils the tasks of the CUS between the Plenary Sessions. It consists of the Chairman of the CUS and the even number of members elected by the Plenary Session of CUS. One-half of the members of the Executive Committee is elected by the delegates of the national sports associations and the second half of the members of the Executive Committee is elected by the delegates of the sports clubs and the sporting unions. For the Executive Committee of CUS to be able to make decisions the majority of its members have to be present and the decisions are then made by the simple majority of these present members. The Executive Committee of CUS is chaired by the Chairman of CUS. The general secretary of CUS and the Chairman of the Revision Committee of CUS have a right to attend the meetings of the Executive Committee. The Executive Committee of CUS has two vice-chairmen, one is elected from the members of the Executive Committee elected by the delegates of the national sports associations and the second one from the members of the Executive Committee elected by the delegates of the sports clubs and the sporting unions. The vice-chairmen are elected by the Executive Committee after the candidates are suggested by the Chairman of CUS.

The Executive Committee of CUS is entitled to make decisions in the following matters:

- to take steps to fulfil the decisions of the Plenary Session of CUS and in the matters connected with the main activity of the CUS according to its statutes;
- to approve and to publish the internal regulations of the CUS, unless these are supposed to be approved by the Plenary Session of CUS according to the Statutes of the CUS;

- to perform the role of the Plenary Sessions of the business corporations owned solely by the CUS;
- to perform the role of a shareholder within business corporations partially owned by the CUS;
- to establish councils, expert committees and similar bodies while determining the members, the goals and the activities of these bodies;
- to ascertain the amounts and due dates of the membership fees;
- to establish the expert centres of the CUS on both national and local level and to directly manage their activities and funding;
- to determine the address of the seat of the CUS in Prague;
- the suggestion to change the Statutes of the CUS regarding solely the additional business activities of the CUS;
- to make decisions regarding the management of the secretariat of the CUS and to establish the general secretary of the CUS.

51. The Council of CUS is the collective representative body of the CUS. It consists of a chairman, two vice-chairmen and the general secretary. All members of the Council of CUS are entitled to represent the CUS separately in all matters in compliance with the decisions of the Plenary Session of CUS and the Executive Committee of CUS.

52. The general secretary is the managing employee of the secretariat of the CUS. The general secretary is in charge of the employees of the CUS and of the activities of the secretariat of the CUS. The general secretary is appointed by the Executive Committee of CUS and participates in all of its meetings.

53. The Revision Committee of CUS is the controlling body of the CUS. It has seven members. The member of the Revision Committee of CUS cannot be simultaneously the member of the Council of CUS or the Executive Committee of CUS and cannot be appointed the liquidator of CUS in case of its termination. The member of the Revision Committee of CUS cannot be in the employer/employee or similar relationship with the CUS. The Revision Committee of CUS is appointed by the Plenary Session of CUS for the time period of four years and the members of the Revision Committee of CUS appoint its chairman and vice-chairman. The Revision Committee of CUS controls and inspects the economic activities of the Executive Committee of CUS, the secretariat of CUS and of the district organizations of CUS. The Revision Committee of CUS is also entitled to carry out inspections of the economic activities connected with the subsidies provided by the CUS to its members.

54. The Honorary Chairman of CUS is the honorary title awarded by the Plenary Session of CUS upon the suggestion of the Executive Committee of CUS to personas with exceptional credit regarding the support and development of sport and its inherent moral, physical, historical and cultural values in the Czech Republic. The Honorary Chairman of CUS is not considered a regular body of the CUS. The Honorary Chairman of CUS is entitled: (i) to participate at the Plenary Session of CUS and upon his request to participate also in the meetings of other bodies of the CUS, (ii) to promote the interests of the CUS according to the decisions of the Plenary Session of CUS and the

Executive Committee of CUS and (iii) to bring suggestions regarding the activities of the CUS to its bodies.

55. Local organizations of the CUS perform the administrative jurisdiction of the CUS matters at the local level according to the regional organizational structure of the CUS. The local organizations are founded as autonomous societies according to the Czech Civil Code and perform their activities in a legally independent way. The statutes of the local organizations of CUS need to be compatible with the basic democratic principles and with the purpose and main activity of the CUS according to its statutes. The local organizations may be founded by the sport clubs and the sport organizations or by the organizational units of the national sport associations active in the local area. In each of the districts according to the regional structure of the CUS only one local organization of the CUS may exist. The local organization becomes a special member of the CUS after being accepted by the Plenary Session of CUS.

Regional organizations of the CUS are founded as subsidiary societies of the CUS, according to the regional organizational structure of the CUS.[52] The name of the organization has to contain the words 'regional organization of the CUS'. The CUS is not responsible for the obligations and debts of its subsidiary societies. The CUS may define the powers and competence of the regional organizations in a more detailed way by an internal regulation approved by the Plenary Session of CUS. The regional organizations are founded and terminated by the decision of the Plenary Session of CUS upon suggestion of the Executive Committee of CUS. The termination of the regional organization may be suggested by the Executive Committee of CUS because of the non-activity of the regional organization, the breach of its statutes, internal regulations or decisions of the bodies of the CUS or because of other serious reason. In case the Plenary Session of CUS decides that the regional organization of the CUS will be terminated it also appoints the liquidator who will be in charge of the liquidation of this regional organization. After the liquidation the remaining financial balance may be used only for the community beneficial purposes.

The purpose of the regional organizations of the CUS is the following:

- to create the local service sport centres and to perform sport activities;
- to perform service activities and to provide services in the area of sport to the members of the CUS and to the general public;
- to perform the administrative jurisdiction of the CUS matters in the region;
- to create conditions to ensure funding of the sport activities in the region with regard to public funds and other possible financial sources;
- to protect the interests of its members and sport in general within the region.

Within its main activity the regional organizations of the CUS especially:

- strive to create the economic, material and legislative conditions to support the development of sport and its members in the region;
- cooperate with regional authorities and municipalities in the area of sport;

52. According to the Ročenka ČUS 2016 (The Yearbook of CUS for 2016), edited by Opatrný, David, Nakladatelství Olympia, Praha, 2017, p. 249, there are fourteen regional organizations of CUS in the Czech Republic.

- protect the interests of its members and general public in the area of sport;
- cooperate with other sport organizations in the region;
- administer their property and protect their legal rights;
- help to organize programmes for development of sport, the education of experts in the area of sport, keep organizing various sport and cultural events;
- according to its possibilities provide various other services for its member entities;
- to support its main activity, the regional organizations of the CUS may also perform additional profitable and business activities.

The members of the regional organization of the CUS may be: (i) the local organization of the CUS active in the region,[53] (ii) the regional subsidiary organizations of national sport associations in case the national sport association is the member of the CUS and (iii) the national sport associations in case they are members of the CUS and they do not have a regional subsidiary organization in the region. The membership is granted and terminated by the Plenary Session of the regional organization of the CUS. The membership in the regional organization of the CUS does not automatically establish the membership within the CUS itself.

The regional organization of the CUS has the following bodies and organs, basically mirroring the structure of the CUS itself:

- the Plenary Session of the regional organization as the supreme body;
- the council of the regional organization as the statutory body;
- the Executive Committee of the regional organization as the executive body;
- the revision Committee of the regional organization as the controlling body.

The authority and activity of the bodies of the regional organizations are established similar to the bodies of the CUS, but are performed on the regional level. The statutes of CUS define the executive activity of the regional organization as activity within the project of the service sports centres established by the Executive Committee of CUS according to the Statutes of the CUS. This executive activity is coordinated by the appointed member of the Executive Committee of CUS.

56. The property and economic assets of the CUS are financial funds, tangible assets, financial receivables, bonds and other property rights. The main sources of financing of the CUS are especially incomes from its own main and additional economic activities, profits of business organizations created by the CUS, subsidies from public funds and donations. The property and economic assets of the CUS are used in compliance with the purpose of the CUS and to support the interests of its members. In case of termination of the CUS the property and economic assets of the CUS are liquidated and settled by the liquidator appointed by the Plenary Session of CUS. The property and economic assets of the terminated CUS will be preferentially offered to the organization with the purpose, status and activities similar to the CUS.

53. According to the official website of the Czech Union of Sports (www.csucz.cz), there are seventy six local organizations of CUS in the Czech Republic.

II. The Society of Sport Associations of the Czech Republic

57. The Society of Sport Associations of the Czech Republic (SSA) is apart from the Czech Olympic Committee and the Czech Union of Sports the third major umbrella sports association active in the area of sport in the Czech Republic. The SSA in its current form developed originally from SVAZARM, the organization active in Czechoslovakia during the communist years. After the change in the regime in 1989, SVAZARM was transformed into the Association of Technical Sports and Activities, which then transformed into the current Society of Sport Associations of the Czech Republic in 2003. The Statutes of the SSA acknowledge that the SSA is the legal successor of SVAZARM and the subsequent association of technical sports and activities. The SSA, identically as its antecedent organizations, unites the national sport associations (currently seventeen national sport associations) managing the sports and activities of technical nature and historically related to defence activities of the state – currently among others: aviation, dog breeding, amateur radio operating, biathlon, scuba diving, motor sport, sport shooting, parachuting, but also the activities of the model makers, firemen, soldiers in reserves and many other mostly outdoor activities. These sport activities are not popular to such extent among the spectators on the mass scale compared to for example some of the most popular sports in the Czech Republic – football and ice hockey, but the SSA still unites more than 600,000 members in almost 10,000 sport clubs in the Czech Republic.[54] As the exception to the rule the popularity of biathlon (one of the member sports of the SSA) has increased dramatically in the last couple of years, the three-day competitions organized by the Czech Biathlon Union in Nové Město na Moravě attracting more than 100,000 visiting spectators.

58. According to its statutes[55] the SSA is the association of legally and financially independent sport clubs and organizations based in the Czech Republic, with their main purpose being the pursuing of sport activities and physical education, the development of sporting and technical abilities and the education of their members and general public in relevant areas. The SSA operates on the whole territory of the Czech Republic and its main purpose is performing the publicly beneficial activity in the area of sport and national defence. The SSA improves conditions for the activities of its members and supports the interests of its members, while in particular especially doing the following:

- supporting the activities and development of its members and providing expert, technical, methodical, legal and other consultancy services;
- organizing sport activities and events;

54. *See* the Annual report of SSA for 2016 at the official website of SSA (www.sporty-cz.cz), http://www.sporty-cz.cz/files/uploads/Soubory/V%C3%BDro%C4%8Dn%C3%AD%20zpr%C3%A1va%202016_Sdru%C5%BEen%C3%AD%20sportovn%C3%ADch%20svaz%C5%AF%20%C4%8Cesk%C3%A9%20republiky,%20z.s.pdf.

55. *See* the current valid and effective Statutes of the Society of Sport Associations approved by the Board of the Society of Sports Associations on 16 Nov. 2017 on the official website of the Czech judiciary: www.justice.cz.

- contributing to development of technical abilities and defence abilities of citizens of the Czech Republic and providing the education towards dealing with crisis situations;
- helping to provide financing for the activities of its members;
- supporting its members in promoting a healthy way of living and preventing negative social trends within the youth;
- representing its members while negotiating with the authorities and municipalities;
- administering its own property and legal rights and if requested the property and legal rights of its members;
- in cooperation with its members cooperating on prevention and liquidation of industrial and ecological accidents, helping in case of natural emergencies and cooperating on protection of the environment;
- protecting and promoting the interests of its members.

To fulfil its tasks, the SSA may also perform additional business and profitable activities with the main purpose of financially supporting its main activities and frugally using its property. Any profit from these additional activities may be used only for the activities of the SSA and its administration.

59. Any person identifying with the purpose and goals of the SSA may become its member after being accepted by the Board of SSA. The Statutes of the SSA recognize three forms of membership with different membership rights and obligations – (i) the regular membership, (ii) the affiliated membership and (iii) the honorary membership. The organizations with its seat at the territory of the Czech Republic may become regular members or affiliated members of the SSA if they agree with the Statutes of the SSA and conclude a contract on cooperation with the SSA. The honorary membership is granted to outstanding personalities and experts in the area of sport and also to legal and natural persons who either actively cooperate with the SSA while not participating directly on its administration or who help to enhance the popularity and good name of the SSA.

The membership rights belonging to all members of the SSA are the following:

- the right to participate on the projects and activities of the SSA and the right to be informed about these projects and activities;
- the right to provide the SSA with suggestions, propositions and incentives regarding its activities;
- the right to be informed about the economic activities of the SSA;
- the right to request information and explanations from the organs and bodies of the SSA.

The honorary members of the SSA have the following rights:

- to participate at the meeting of the Board of SSA personally or to send their representative to this meeting;
- to nominate and be nominated as candidates into the organs and bodies of the SSA.

Every member of the SSA has the following obligations:

- to maintain and protect the interests of the SSA and to help fulfil the goals of the SSA;
- to protect the good name of the SSA;
- to abide by the Statutes of the SSA.

The membership in the SSA may be terminated in the following ways:

- By a written notice of the member organization about its withdrawal from the SSA decided in accordance with the statutes of this member organization. The written notice should be delivered to the Board of SSA at least three months prior to the termination of the membership of the member organization.
- By the exclusion of a member of the SSA for a serious breach of the Statutes of the SSA or serious damage to the interests of the SSA.
- By a legal termination of a membership entity of the SSA.

60. The SSA has the following bodies and organs:

- The Board of SSA as the supreme body.
- The Control Committee of SSA as the controlling body.
- The Chairman of SSA and the Vice-Chairmen of SSA as the representatives of the SSA.

61. The Board of SSA consists of the representatives of the member sport associations (one representative per association) and of the Chairman of SSA. Every representative has one vote and for the Board of SSA to be able to vote, at least two-thirds of the representatives must be present. Decisions are made by the simple majority of the representatives. The quorum of two-thirds of all the representatives is necessary for the budget of the SSA and the election rules to be approved and also to elect the Chairman of the SSA or to remove him from the office. Some of the crucial decisions regarding the purpose and activity of the SSA need to be approved by all member associations. These are the decisions regarding the change of Statutes of the SSA, the legal changes regarding the subsidiary organizations of the SSA, decisions about the membership fees, decisions regarding the business activities of SSA and decisions regarding the exclusion of the member association of the SSA.

The Board of SSA is authorized to decide in the following matters:

- approving the Statutes of the SSA, the symbolic of the SSA and the rules of order of the SSA and any changes of these regulations;
- electing and removing the Chairman of SSA and the Vice-Chairmen of SSA from their offices;
- deciding on admission of a new member organization and on the exclusion of the current member organization of the SSA;
- making decisions regarding the membership fees and their amounts;
- approving the budget and the accounts of the SSA;

- following the proposal of the Chairman of SSA approving the organizational structure of the secretariat of SSA;
- electing the representatives of SSA to negotiate with other organizations public and private;
- deciding in economic matters and regarding the secretariat of the SSA;
- approving the Statute of the Control Committee of SSA, the election of its members and the annual reports of the Control Committee of SSA;
- deciding on establishing business corporations or acquiring shares in business corporations and matters of business relationships regarding the SSA's additional business activities;
- deciding on beginning and concluding of the SSA's business activities;
- deciding all the matters regarding the establishing, termination and transformation of the subsidiary organizations of the SSA;
- establishing the expert committees, working groups and other bodies of the SSA and approves the chairmen of these bodies and committees;
- determining the extent of the coordination and service activities of the SSA;
- creating suitable conditions for the activities and development of the SSA and its member organizations;
- electing and removing the representatives of the SSA in regions.

62. The Control Committee of SSA is the control and revision body of the SSA. The Statute of the Control Committee of SSA is approved by the Board of SSA. The Control Committee has three to five members delegated usually by different member organizations of the SSA and approved by the Board of SSA for the term of five years. The members of the Committee elect the Chairman and the Vice-Chairman of the Committee. The Chairman of the Control Committee of SSA is allowed to participate at the meetings of the Board of SSA with the advisory vote.

63. The Chairman and the Vice-Chairmen of the SSA are the statutory representatives of SSA, each of them enabled to represent the SSA and to act on its behalf independently. The Chairman of the SSA summons and chairs the meeting of the Board of SSA. In the time period between the meetings of the Board of SSA the chairman decides all matters regarding the member organizations, except those exclusively decided by the Board of SSA. The chairman is elected by the Board of the SSA for the term of five years and answers to the Board of SSA. The position of the chairman is not compatible with the position of the chairman of any of the member organizations of SSA. The vice-chairmen are elected by the Board of SSA from its members for the term of five years and their activities within the SSA are coordinated by the chairman.

64. By the decision of the Board of SSA the SSA may establish its subsidiary organizations with their legal status derived from the SSA. The statutes of these subsidiary organizations of SSA establish their internal structure and have to be compatible with the statutes of SSA. The membership within the subsidiary organization of the SSA automatically established the membership within the SSA. The SSA is not responsible for the debts of its subsidiary organizations. The main sources of financing of the SSA are especially subsidies from public funds and donations, incomes from its service activities, donations from sponsors, membership fees, profits from the property owned by the SSA and from the business activities of the SSA.

The Statutes of the SSA also state that apart from the fusion with another organization or dissolution by the decision of the Board of SSA or by the decision of courts, the SSA is automatically terminated in case the number of membership organization is less than three. In case of the termination of the SSA the appointed liquidator will liquidate the remaining property of the SSA.

Chapter 2. Public Regulation

§1. Fundamental Rights

I. The Constitution and Sport

65. The two basic constitutional acts of the Czech Republic – the Act No. 1/1993 Coll., the Constitution of the Czech Republic and the Act No. 2/1993 Coll., the Charter of fundamental rights and freedoms – do not mention sport in any way, therefore we may declare that in the Czech Republic sport is non-constitutional[56] as the right for sport or the guarantee of sporting activities is part of neither the constitution nor the charter of fundamental rights and freedoms.[57] The Charter of fundamental rights and freedoms is part of the constitutional order[58] of the Czech Republic and is considered the core of the democratic Constitution of the Czech Republic, while listing the inherent, inalienable, imprescriptible and irrevocable rights that belong to every citizen of the Czech Republic.[59]

66. The existence of the sport organizations and the sport clubs may be considered a typical execution of the right of association according to the Article 20 section 1 of the Charter of fundamental rights and freedoms, which guarantees the right of free and unrestricted association and the right to join organizations, clubs or other associations in its Article 20 in the following way:[60]

(1) The right of association is guaranteed. Everybody has the right to associate together with others in clubs, societies, and other associations.
(2) Citizens also have the right to form political parties and political movements and to associate therein.
(3) The exercise of these rights may be limited only in cases specified by law, if it involves

56. In states where sport and the right for sport is explicitly mentioned in the Constitution, we consider sport as being constitutional. For more on this classification of law see Various Authors: Sportovní právo (Sports law): Chapter 3 – 'Sport norms and other non-legal sources of rules of athlete's behaviors' by Sup, Martin, Auditorium, Praha, 2012, p. 52 and Králík, Michal: Právo ve sportu (Law in Sport), C.H. Beck, Praha, 2001, pp. 172 et seq.
57. *See* Kubíček, Jiří: Sport a právo (Sport and Law), Masarykova univerzita, Brno, 2012, p. 58.
58. Apart from the Constitution and the Charter of fundamental rights and freedoms the constitutional order of Czech Republic contains additional constitutional acts and several international agreements regarding the human rights and freedoms ratified by Czech Republic.
59. *See* Art no. 1 of the Act. No 2/1993 Coll., the Charter of fundamental rights and freedoms. On possible restriction of these rights see ZOUBEK, Vladimír: Postmoderní problémy lidských práv a globální bezpečnosti (Postmodern Problems of Human Rights and Global Security), Aleš Čeněk, Plzeň, 2004, pp. 198 et seq.
60. *See* Art 20 of the Act No. 2/1993 Coll., the Charter of fundamental rights and freedoms.

measures that are necessary in a democratic society for the security of the state, the protection of public security and public order, the prevention of crime, or the protection of the rights and freedoms of others.

(4) Political parties and political movements, as well as other associations, are separate from the state.

§2. Special Sports Legislation

I. The Act on Support of Sport

67. The Act on Support of Sport[61] passed in 2001 is considerably brief containing only several paragraphs and even though recently amended, in comparison with the above-mentioned Slovakian legislation seems ridiculously outdated. The novelization[62] effective since 1 January 2017, however, focused mainly on bringing more transparency into the process of the financial support of sports organizations, thus creating the below described electronic register of sports organizations and bringing several other changes without seriously updating the legal framework of sport in general.

68. According to its paragraph 1, the Act on Support of Sport defines the role of sport within society in very general way and determines the tasks of ministries, regional and local authorities in connection with the support of sport. The last novelization effective since 1 January 2017 has added the new paragraph 1a according to which the main priorities within the area of support of sport in the Czech Republic are: (i) the support of sporting activities of youth and children and their trainers and coaches and (ii) the support of the athletes representing the Czech Republic internationally.

69. The paragraph 2 section 1 of the Act on Support of Sport contains the definition of sport as:

> … all forms of physical activity which, through casual or organised participation, aim at expressing or improving the physical fitness and mental well-being, forming social relationships, maintaining health or obtaining results in competition at all levels, individually or collectively.[63]

This definition of sport has too been amended by the recent novelization, which has broadened the term by including *the casual activities* and also mentioned *the individual and collective factor* at the end of the definition. Apart from the definition of sport the paragraph 2 also contains the definitions of the following other terms:

61. *See* the Act No. 11/2001 Coll., in support of sport, as amended.
62. *See* the Act No. 230/2016 Coll., which amends the Act No. 115/2001 Coll., on support of sport.
63. This definition is very similar to the definition of sport in the White Paper on Sport, presented by European Commission on 11 Jul. 2007 in Brussels, being the definition of sport from the Council of Europe Sport's Charter adopted in 1992.

(1) *the sports organization* – a new term defined as a legal person founded with a purpose other than making a profit in case this legal person performs activities in the area of sport;
(2) *the athlete* – any natural person who really performs sport activities, while being registered with any sports organization during a calendar year;
(3) *the sport for everyone* – organized and non-organized sporting and physical activities designated for the general public;
(4) *the sports facilities* – the premises – estate, body of water or complex used exclusively or predominantly for sport activities;
(5) *the important sport event* – the sport event of international importance taking place in the territory of Czech Republic (for example the races of the IBU Biathlon World Cup programme which regularly take place in Nové Město na Moravě);
(6) *the significant sport event with extraordinary importance* – the sport event of international importance taking place in the territory of Czech Republic which is assigned to a particular state under the condition that the state proclaims that it shall ensure the conditions for this sporting event (these are the sport events of the worldwide impact, such as Olympic Games, FIFA World Cup).

These legal definitions however are too vague and too shallow to create the concepts and institutions relevant and necessary for the modern sports legal framework.

70. The following paragraph no. 3 of the Act on Support of Sport defines the tasks of the Ministry of Education, Youth and Sport, the most important of the central bodies of state administration connected with sport. Within the area of support of sport in the Czech Republic the Ministry of Education, Youth and Sport has the following tasks:

- to prepare the draft of the plan of the state's sport policy to be approved by the Government of the Czech Republic – this plan determines the goals of the State's Policy within the area of sport and the priorities and standards of the support of sport from the state's budget. The plan of the state's sport policy contains the steps and arrangements against match-fixing and competition-fixing and the arrangements to support the education and further professional career of the former athletes who represented the Czech Republic following the end of their professional sport careers;
- to coordinate the practical steps while following the plan of the state's sport policy approved by the government;
- to ensure the financial support of sport from the state's budget;
- to control the use of public funds and subsidies from the state's budget used in sport and the control of recipients of these funds and subsidies;
- to create conditions for the sport activities of youth and children and their coaches and trainers, for the development of sport for everyone, for the sport and activities of the physically handicapped and for the athletes representing the Czech Republic at the sport events in the Czech Republic and abroad;
- to issue the anti-doping programme in the Czech Republic and to organize and to ensure the fulfilment of this programme and to issue the programme against match-fixing and competition-fixing;

- to establish the contribution-based organization of the ministry to ensure the fulfilment of obligations arising from the International Convention against Doping in Sport;
- to establish the resort sports centre and to ensure its activity;
- to coordinate the activities of the resort sport centres of the Ministry of Defence and the Ministry of Interior;
- to maintain the electronic register of sports organizations requesting financial support from state's budget, and of athletes, trainers and coaches and sports facilities financed from the state's budget.

71. Paragraph 4 of the Act on Support of Sport mentions the tasks of the other central bodies of the state administration. The Ministry of Defence and the Ministry of Interior within their authority create the conditions for the development of sport, for the preparation of the state's representation and for the development if the talented athletes, establish their own resort sports centres and ensure their activities. The Ministry of Health within its authority organizes the medical services provided for the athletes representing the Czech Republic and for the talented youth, creates organizational conditions enabling a specific access of the athletes to the clinical care and to support the healthy lifestyle and creates conditions to support the preventive, periodical and consultative health care in the area of sport.

72. The above-mentioned electronic register is a major addition to the Act on Support of Sport brought by the last novelization of this act effective from 1 January 2017. According to the explanatory memorandum to the novelization of Act on Support of Sport the electronic register should help the government and the ministries analyse and evaluate the state's policies in the area of sport, which should be subsequently properly adjusted or regulated based on the information provided by the register. In the future the register should provide valuable information with regard to the number of members of the particular sport organization or the development of the membership base of a particular sport organization through time, etc.[64] The electronic register is described in the next paragraph 3a of the Act on Support of Sport as the informative system of the public administration created for gathering information regarding the sports organizations, the athletes and the sports facilities. The administrator of the register is the Ministry of Education, Youth and Sport. The register is non-public, with the exception of the information on the number of athletes and trainers registered with a particular sports organization, which should be accessible to the general public. The sports organization requesting the financial support from the state's budget according to the following paragraph 6b or 6c shall enter into the register the following information regarding these organization (including the subsequent changes of these information) – the name of the organization, its registered seat, its identification number, its main activity and its activity within the area of sport, the membership in any other sports organization, the termination of the sports organization's activity within the area of sport and the date of this termination, the information regarding the organization which is the member of the original organization, the information (the name, surname, date of birth, address and dates regarding the beginning and end of the sport activity)

64. *See* the explanatory memorandum to the Act No. 230/2016 Coll., which amends the Act No. 115/2001 Coll., on support of sport.

regarding the athletes and trainers registered with this membership organization and with the original organization, the sports facilities the sport organization is using for its activities and activities of its members including the information on the subsidies from the state's budget provided in connection with these sports facilities. Within the electronic register the sports organization has access to information regarding the athletes and trainers registered with this organization and its member organizations. The Ministry of Education, Youth and Sport as the administrator of the electronic register authenticates the truthfulness, comprehensiveness and correctness of the information in the register. The Ministry of Interior provides the Ministry of Education, Youth and Sport with referential data from the basic register of citizens[65] (names, surnames, dates and places of birth, addresses, dates of death, nationality, numbers of the identity cards) to enable it to perform its administrator role.

73. According to the temporary provisions of the novelization, the Ministry of Education, Youth and Sport shall put the electronic register into operation within eighteen months since the effectiveness of the novelization of the Act on Support of Sport, i.e. before 30 June 2019. According to the temporary provisions the sports organizations with other membership sports organizations is obliged to enter the obligatory information into the register within twenty-four months since the effectiveness of the novelization of the Act on Support of sport, i.e. before 31 December 2019. The other sports organizations are obliged to enter the obligatory information into the register within thirty months since the effectiveness of the novelization of the Act on Support of sport, i.e. before 30 June 2020. The failure to enter the information or the change of the relevant information regarding the sports organization into the electronic register is considered an offence according to the paragraph 7d section 2 and the following of the Act on Support of Sport. The proceedings are held by the Ministry of Education, Youth and Sport and the ministry may sanction the sports organization by a fine up to CZK 100,000.[66]

74. The following paragraphs nos 5 and 6 of the Act on Support of Sport contain the tasks of the regional and local administrations. Both regional and local administrations create conditions for sport within their area of competence, mainly: (i) to ensure the development of sport for everyone and the development of the talented youth and the physically handicapped, (ii) to ensure the financial support of development of sport from their financial budgets, (iii) to ensure the construction, reconstruction, maintenance and running of sports facilities within their area. The local administrations also control the effective use of the sports facilities within the area. The regional administrations additionally prepare the plan of development of sport within the region and ensure its implementation. The local administration prepares the plan for development of sport on the local level within its area of self-governance and ensure its implementation. The plan of development of sport within the region and on the local level shall contain the definition of the areas of support of sport, the priorities within the specified areas and the steps and arrangements to be taken towards ensuring the accessibility of the sports facilities for the general public. The plan of development of sport within the region and on the local level shall also include the determination of the financial funds out of the regional or local budget, which should be used for the implementation of

65. *See* the Act No. 133/2000 Coll., on the evidence of citizens and on birth numbers, as amended.
66. Approximately EUR 4,000.

the plan. As mentioned in the explanatory memorandum to the novelization of the Act on Support of Sport effective since 1 January 2017, the more transparent allocation of these financial funds is the main purpose of these new stipulations included by the last novelization of the Act on Support of Sport.[67] The regional and local administrations are obliged to prepare the above-mentioned plans within eighteen months since the effectiveness of the novelization, i.e. before 30 June 2019.

75. The financial support of sport is described in the paragraph 6b of the Act on Support of Sport. The Ministry of Education, Youth and Sport provides the support of sport from the state's budget in the form of subsidies within various programmes declared for every calendar year, focused mainly on the support of sport activities of the children and youth, the support of sport for everyone, the support of sport of the physically handicapped and the support of the top performing athletes representing the Czech Republic. Following the execution of the electronic register of sport organizations operated by the Ministry of Education, Youth and Sport, the subsidies may only be allocated to those sport organizations that have entered the requested information into this register. The Ministry of Education, Youth and Sport within a special programme also provides the support of sport from the state's budget in the form of subsidies for acquirement or technical revaluation of tangible and intangible long-term property. The support of sport in the form of subsidies may not be allocated to a person, who has repeatedly committed anti-doping regulation violations or has breached the anti-doping rules in a serious way, to a person who has endangered the implementation of the programme of prevention of match-fixing and competition-fixing, or to a person who has been legally effectively convicted of a crime connected with sport or of a crime of subsidy fraud, unless the convictions of this person has been legally deleted. As mentioned above, any sports organization requesting the support from public funds is obliged to enter the information about this sports organization into the electronic register or to change the relevant information regarding the sports organization according to the reality in the electronic register. The failure to enter the information regarding the sports facility (address, description of the facility and the amount of financial support allocated from public funds and the purpose of the use of this financial support) is considered an offence according to the paragraph 7d section 7 of the Act on Support of Sport. The proceedings are held by the Ministry of Education, Youth and Sport and the ministry may sanction the sports organization by a fine up to CZK 100,000.[68]

76. Based on the approval of the Government of Czech Republic, the central bodies of government create suitable conditions for the organization of significant sporting events of extraordinary importance in the territory of the Czech Republic. The request for approval by the government is submitted by the candidate party for the organization of the event through the Ministry of Education, Youth and Sport. The above-mentioned request for approval contains the anticipated cost estimate of the event and the study regarding workability of the event's organization specifying the necessary measures and arrangements to be made by the public authorities in connection

---

67. *See* also the article 'Novela zákona o podpoře sportu' ('The Amendment to the Act on Support of Sport') by JUDr. Jiří Janák and Mgr. Jan Urban, published on 27 Jan. 2017 at www.epravo.cz, https://www.epravo.cz/top/clanky/novela-zakona-o-podpore-sportu-104847.html.

68. Approximately EUR 4,000.

with the organization of the event especially in the areas of security, protection of health and life, human resources, residence of foreigners on the territory of the Czech Republic and traffic accessibility. The study shall also contain the information regarding the public funds necessary for the organization of the event and whether this use of public funds would be in compliance with the principle of economical, effective and efficient use of public funds. The study shall also contain the information regarding the sustainability of the operation of the sports facilities and general infrastructure built in connection with the organization of the sports event. The financial support out of the state's budget for the organization of significant sporting events of extraordinary importance approved by the Government of Czech Republic is provided mainly by the Ministry of Education, Youth and Sport. The other important sport events are financially supported from the subsidy programmes provided by the Ministry of Education, Youth and Sport as described in the paragraph 6b of the Act on Support of Sport.[69] The Ministry of Education, Youth and Sport coordinates the providing of the financial support according to the Act on Support of Sport with the Office for the Protection of Competition.[70] The financial support cannot be granted in case such support is incompatible with the conditions on providing the public support determined by the European Union's laws or with the decision of the European Commission based on these laws.

77. According to the paragraph 7a of the Act on Support of Sport, the owner of the sports facility or the person allowed to use the sports facility to organize a sports

69. In 2017 the Ministry of Youth, Education and Sport provided in total ten programmes in which sports organizations could have requested financial support from the state's budget under different conditions and for different support. (i) Programme no 1. – Representation (in this programme only the national sports associations ma request funds to finance accommodation of the athletes and staff at the international sports events, travelling expenses or technical service; (ii) Programme no. 2 - Youth (in this programme the national sports association may request funds to support the talented youth not older than 23 years); (iii) Programme no. 3 – Sports Organizations (in this programme all sports organizations may request funds for their operational costs); (iv) Programme no. 4 – The Maintenance and Operation of the Sports Facilities (in this programme the sports organizations may request funds to pay operational costs like electricity or heating); (v) Programme no. 5 – Sports Associations (in this programme the national sports association may request funds for its operational costs); (vi) Programme no 6 – Sports Events (in this programme the sports organizations may request funds to support their events, the funds are allocated based upon the importance of the event; (vii) Programme no. 7 – Handicapped athletes (this programme is used for the support of sport activities of the handicapped athletes); (viii) Programme no. 8 – Sport Clubs – non-investment funds (in this programme the sports clubs may request funds based on the number of their members to cover their operational costs); (ix) Programme no. 9 – Sport at Schools and Universities (this programme is used to support the sports at schools and universities); (x) Programme no. 10 – Sporting Activities of the general public (in this programme the national sports organizations may request funds for propagation and organization of the sporting activities for the general public.

70. The Office for the Protection of Competition is the state's central body of governance concerned with the support and protection of the economic competition. The Office has its seat in Brno and is governed by the apolitical chairman appointed by the president of Czech Republic for the time limit of six years after being suggested by the government Of Czech Republic. Its scope of authority was established by the Act No. 273/1996 Coll., on the scope of authority of the Office of the Protection of Competition.

event, i.e. the operator of the sports facility, are obliged, in case it is necessary for the security of people and property within the sports facility, to make all the necessary arrangements to ensure order during the sports events and to issue the visitors rules, containing mainly the rules regarding the entering the sports facility for the spectators and rules regarding the organizing service modified according to the local conditions. In case the security of the people or the property is threatened in serious way within the sports facility and despite all the measures and arrangements taken by the owner or the operator of the sports facility the order is not restored, the owner and the operator are obliged to initiate the termination of the ongoing sports event and request the cooperation of the Police of the Czech Republic. In case the serious threat against the security of people or property appears without the owner or the operator making all the necessary arrangements to restore order during the sports events, and the Police of the Czech Republic is forced to restore the order, the Police of the Czech Republic is entitled to receive the compensation of the costs spent in connection with its actions. The above-mentioned obligations of the owner and operator of the sports facility are inspected by the local authorities. In case the owner or the operator of the sports facility violates his obligation to make all the necessary arrangements to ensure order during the sports events, the Ministry of Interior is entitled to decide that the particular sports event will be taking place without the spectators for the maximum time period of one year. The proceedings leading to the decision of the Ministry of Interior can be initiated by the request of the local authority or by the decision of the Ministry of Interior itself. The Ministry of Interior may shorten the time period of the sanction according to the previous sentence based on the request of the owner or the operator of the sports facility, who successfully proves that measures and arrangements necessary to ensure the security of people and property within the sports facility has taken place. The Ministry of Interior supervises the realization of the awarded sanction. The above-mentioned obligations arising from the Act of Support of Sport do not concern the owner of the sports facilities in case these obligations have been transferred to the operator of the sports facility.

78. The owner or the operator of the sports facility commits an offence according to the Act on Support of Sport by not issuing the visitors rules or by not making these visitors rules public and for this may be awarded a fine up to CZK 100,000[71] (in case of the natural person who does not do business up to CZK 50,000). The owner or the operator commits an offence according to the Act on Support of Sport by not initiating the termination of the ongoing sports event or by not requesting the cooperation of the Police of Czech Republic in case the security of the people or the property is threatened in a serious way within the sports facility and despite all the measures and arrangements taken by the owner or the operator of the sports facility the order is not restored and for this may be awarded a fine up to CZK 1,000,000[72] (in case of natural person who does not do business up to CZK 500,000). The owner or the operator of the sports facility commits an offence according to the Act on Support of Sport by ignoring the decision of the Ministry of Interior that the sports event shall take place without the spectators and for this may be awarded a fine up to CZK 2,000,000[73] (in

71. Approximately EUR 4,000.
72. Approximately EUR 40,000.
73. Approximately EUR 80,000.

case of natural person who does not do business up to CZK 1,000,000). The local authorities are authorized to decide the offences of the owners or operators of the sports facilities, award sanctions and collect fines awarded for these offences.

79. The Act on Support of Sport also contains a special provision regarding the expropriation[74] of the sports facilities (building, estate, its complex or other facilities built or used for sports activities). In case of expropriation of the sports facilities the Act on Support of Sport presupposes that the owner of the expropriated sports facilities may receive compensation in kind, i.e. other sports facilities in the comparable extent and quality.[75]

§3. Criminal and Civil Liability for Injuries in Sport

80. The Czech criminal law does not contain any specific provisions with regard to the area of amateur or professional sport. Naturally, there is no doubt that the law covers whatever happens on the pitch no matter whether the well-paid professional or amateurs are playing. However, with no specific provisions regarding torts in the area of sport and with the predominant typical presumption that sport is covered by its own rules, there have been too few court decisions to establish a consistent deciding practice especially in the area of sports-related injuries.

81. Recently however, there has been a decision of the Supreme Court of Czech Republic regarding the injury sustained in the match of one of the amateur football competitions in Prague, where one of the players tackled his opponent with the ball recklessly from behind and broke his ankle and his wrist, resulting in operation and approximately three months of recovery out of work. Following the ruling of the courts that what happened was not a criminal offence, the public prosecutor appealed to the Supreme Court of Czech Republic, which in one of the most important decisions[76] connected with the area of sport in the history of the Czech Republic summarized the previous scarce decisions of the Czech courts regarding sport, while also indicating a new direction in decision-making in the area of criminal liability in sport, stating the following:

– apart from ensuring the fairness of the competition and the balanced conditions for participants, one of the purposes of the rules of the game (sport rules) is to protect the health of the athletes against tackles and hits which could lead to injuries;

---

74. For the general legislation regarding expropriation see the Act No. 184/2006 Coll., on revocation and restriction of property rights to lands and buildings (Expropriation Act).
75. This is slightly different from the general stipulations on expropriation according to the Act No. 184/2006 Coll., on revocation and restriction of property rights to lands and buildings (the Expropriation Act), as the general stipulations presume that the compensation will be provided primarily in financial funds and the compensation in kind (for example provision of comparable land in case of expropriation of land) can be provided only in case of agreement between the owner and the expropriator.
76. *See* the resolution of the Supreme Court of Czech Republic No. 7 Tdo 561/2016, dated 31 Aug. 2016.

- the injuries of athletes sustained during sport activities need to be considered in strictly individual and specific way with regard to the specifics of the particular sport and to the extent of the breach of the rules of the game;
- only after this strictly individual and specific consideration it may be decided whether the injury of the athlete remains within the rules of the game or whether the criminal law or civil liability in this particular case needs to be applied.
- following the above-mentioned reasoning the crucial statement with regard to the criminal or civil liability of athletes is *that the breach of the rules of the game (sport rules) does not automatically lead to criminal or civil liability*;
- furthermore, the principle of subsidiarity of the criminal sanctioning should be respected and the criminal law should be applied in case of an excess out of the rules of the game, i.e. in case of intentional or even negligent conduct that seriously breaches the rules of the game and as such is not even sanctioned by the rules of the game (with regard to the consequences to the health of the injured person). For the breach of the rules of the game to be considered excessive, the conduct should be in obvious deviation from the usual means of playing the game;
- in this case the nature of football as a quick contact game means that the excess should be more intensive than the usual tackle happening regularly within the game, as the unfortunate consequence of this tackle (serious injury) of the player cannot be the only means to determining whether there has been an excess out of the rules of the game or not.

82. The majority of legal theory in the Czech Republic is of the opinion that the above-mentioned decision of the Supreme Court of Czech Republic has directed the court decision-making in the area of the criminal responsibility within sport in the Czech Republic[77] towards the European legal trend in this area, mostly by acknowledging that not every breach of the rules of the game leads to criminal liability. The criminal liability takes part only in case of an excess out of the rules of the game, i.e. in case the player exceeds the usual culture of the game. The conduct of the athlete that is considered as being within the rules of the game may subsequently be punished by the Disciplinary Regulations of the particular national sports association.

83. The above described decision of the Supreme Court of Czech Republic is equally important in the area of the civil liability regarding the injuries arising from sports. Apart from the general conditions of the existence of Constitution of the liability for damages according to the Czech law,[78] the courts shall in the future always consider whether the breach of sports rules in each particular case was an excess out of the rules of game (or out of the so-called culture of the game).

---

77. To learn more about the evolution of the criminal liability of athletes for injuries in sport including the present trends see various literature by the Supreme Court justice Michal Králík, who has been focusing on the area of liability of athletes and the area of sports in general for a long time, especially: Králík, Michal: Civilní a trestní odpovědnost sportovců za sportovní úrazy (The civil and criminal liability of athletes in case of sports injuries), Nakladatelství Leges, Praha, 2016 or many of his articles on this topic published in various legal periodicals, for example Jurisprudence, Bulletin advokacie, Soudní rozhledy, etc.
78. These are: (i) unlawful conduct, (ii) existence of damages, (iii) causal link between the unlawful conduct and the existence of damages, (iv) culpability of the person who caused the damage.

§4. The Legal Aspects of Security at the Sporting Events

84. The attendance at the matches of the first professional football league varies, with the average number oscillating around 5,000 visitors per match, however some clubs have the average attendance of ten thousand spectators per home match.[79] In the first ice hockey league the average number of visitors is slightly above the 5,000 per match. As the clubs are always trying to find ways to improve the attendance, truth is that all the professional clubs struggle with the security at their stadiums, all the more so when in the Czech Republic extremely followed and popular matches are being played (e.g. derby Sparta – Slavia with long historical tradition) in front of the stadium-capacity audience. Again we may note that there is no special legislation concerning the security matters regarding the mass attended events in professional sport, only general obligations of the owner of the sports facilities incorporate in the Act on Support of Sport. We may not only find the reason for this in historical development of law in the Czech Republic, but also in the fact that in the Czech Republic there has never been a tragedy at the sporting event comparable to tragedies that happened at football events in Europe (e.g. Glasgow in 1971, Brussels in 1985 or Hillsborough in 1989), therefore the political will to adopt a special legislation to prevent such tragedies in this area has never actually existed.

85. In practice, the most paralyzing aspect for the clubs is the lack of authority of the members of the security or stewards present at the stadium. The members of the security are not entitled to request the identification of the misbehaving fans at the stadium, according to the law they are only entitled to detain these fans until the arrival of the Police of Czech Republic. Given that the Police is often not present at the stadiums this is highly impractical. In case of an attack from the fans, the members of the security and stewards are not protected by the law in any special way. In practice, the legal institute of necessary defence[80] is being used, which is problematic and gives the security and stewards no real authority with the fans.

86. The fans are mostly aware that in case of misbehaviour at the stadium they would not be punished in any serious way. Their behaviour is often disproportionally to its dangerousness at the stadium classified as a minor offence[81] and sanctioned by a small fine. Exceptionally, when their conduct is classified as a criminal offence (usually one in six cases identified by the Police), the individual fans may be banned from entering the stadium.[82] However, the impact of this sanction in general is questionable. The professional clubs mostly agree that trying to ban the most problematic fans who repeatedly misbehave at stadiums is the only way to make the stadiums safe, however they often do not have enough information about the fans that have been banned from their stadium and getting this information from the Police or other authorities is often problematic, because the club has to prove its legitimate interest in this information. The efforts of FACR and other subjects to create a functioning

79. The detailed statistics regarding the attendance are available at the official website of the top professional football league in Czech Republic: www.hetliga.cz.
80. *See* § 29 of the Act No. 40/2009 Coll., the criminal code, as amended.
81. *See* Act No. 251/2016 Coll., on particular offences, as amended.
82. The ban on visiting sports, cultural and other events according to § 76 of Act No. 40/2009, the criminal code, as amended.

database of problematic fans that have been punished by the courts in the past have been unsuccessful so far.

87. The suggestion of the Ministry of Interior that the clubs should impose their own bans on misbehaving fans is problematic in several ways. In practice, the Czech clubs usually have no technical way of enforcing that the banned fan will not get into the stadium – for this a quality camera system with the database of pictures of the banned fans is necessary, or a strict policy of selling the tickets only to holders of the club cards or a similar policy leading to identification of all fans that may enter the stadium. The clubs usually try to avoid the measures pressing all the fans for identification, as due to historical reasons the general public in the Czech Republic is very sensitive about providing others with their personal information, and the clubs are worried that this may lead to a continuous lowering of the attendance at the stadiums.

88. With regard to the security at the stadiums, the Ministry of Interior[83] promotes the concept of the 'lord of the house' which basically means that the relationship between the club and the fan is governed by the private law and therefore the club as the owner of the stadium may determine the rules of behaviour by the written visitors' rules at the stadium and the fan should abide by these rules, accepting the sanctions, fines and contractual penalties. However, the 'lord of the house' concept is not a legal term and is not enshrined in any of the Czech laws, which makes some of the measures of the club based on this concept legally problematic and in theory vulnerable against the legal action from the fans. It also makes the club potentially vulnerable to restrictions from the authorities, mainly with regard to the laws on protection of consumers, as the relationship between the club and the fans falls under the Act on Protection of the Consumer.[84]

89. The football clubs are often sanctioned for the behaviour of their fans, traditionally at their home stadium, but more recently also while playing away matches.[85] The Disciplinary Committee of the League Football Association, the body in charge of hearing the disciplinary offences in Czech professional football usually imposes a fine, or in more serious cases other sanctions (closing of the specific sector at the stadium, the next match being played behind closed doors, etc.). The similar type of sanctions is often imposed on clubs participating in the UEFA Europa League and UEFA Champions League by the UEFA Disciplinary Committee. Of course the fines imposed in the UEFA competitions are many times higher than in the Czech domestic competitions.[86] However, the clubs are not able to sue the fans for damages to compensate

83. *See* Manuál pro fotbalové kluby – právní aspekty bezpečnosti na stadionech v souvislosti s řešením diváckého násilí (The Handbook for football clubs – the legal aspects of the security at stadiums in connection with the question of the spectator violence), Ministerstvo Vnitra České Republiky, 2015. The handbook prepared by the Ministry of Interior summarizes the legal possibilities of clubs with regard to security at the stadiums and tries to offer solutions by applying the general laws. Available at http://www.mvcr.cz/clanek/ministerstvo-vnitra-predstavilo-manual-pro-fotbalove-kluby.aspx.

84. *See* Act No. 634/1992 Coll., on protection of the consumer, as amended.

85. *See* §§ 65 and 66 of the Disciplinary Regulations of FACR available at the official website of FACR: (www.fotbal.cz), https://facr.fotbal.cz/uredni-deska-predpisy/195?category=1.

86. *See* UEFA Disciplinary Regulations (Edition 2017) at the official website of UEFA: (www.uefa.com), https://www.uefa.com/MultimediaFiles/Download/Regulations/uefaorg/UEFACompDisCases/02/48/23/06/2482306_DOWNLOAD.pdf.

for this fine caused by the fans' behaviour for several reasons. The first problem is the formulation of the decision containing the sanction as the club is usually sanctioned for the breach of its own obligations (e.g. sanction for the breach of the obligations of the organizing club) making the causal link between the behaviour of the fans and the sanction to the club difficult to establish. The second problem is that the club usually has no legal instruments to identify the misbehaving fans other than the cooperation with the Police which is not always possible. And even if the club successfully identifies some of the fans, it is difficult to determine the proportion of the damage this fans has caused as the fine is usually imposed for the generally defined crowd behaviour (mass chanting, fireworks, etc.).

90. Several professional clubs in Czech Republic have tried to compensate for this by adopting specifically defined contractual penalties in case of a specific misbehaviour of fans at the stadiums into their visitors' rules (fireworks, racist chanting, etc.). In case the Police successfully identify the perpetrator, the club will then try to sue the perpetrator for the contractual penalty at the general court. Should the courts accept this legal argumentations arising from the theoretical legal concept of 'the lord of the house', thus may prove to be a partial solution to the situations. However, the first final decisions of the courts are yet to come.

Part II. Sport and Employment

§1. Historical Background

91. The major change of the legal status of athletes in the Czech Republic[87] took place after the so-called *Velvet Revolution* of 1989. Until that, the legal position of athletes was not formally professional. With regard to the socialist state system and political line at that time, athletes were employed in state-owned companies. However, they were just purely formal employees, they actually practiced sporting activities; the employment was just '*cover*'. The exception to the rule were the tennis players and also in the short period prior to *Velvet Revolution* in November 1989 the football and ice hockey players. There was no *professionalism* in the current sense of the word. The breakthrough was the year 1989, more precisely the mentioned *Velvet Revolution*, when the new possibilities of legal status of athletes and respective sports activities were opened. Starting with the year 1989, we can talk about the full professionalization of sport and the subsequent search for the appropriate legal status of an athlete.

92. Currently there is no special legal regulation in the Czech Republic determining the legal status or the position of a professional athlete. Although there is the above described Act on Support of Sport,[88] the legal frame in the Czech Republic in this regard is obviously not sufficient. The Act on Support of Sport determines – in a declarative way – the position of the sport in society as a public benefit activity and sets out the tasks of ministries, other administrative authorities and the competence of territorial self-governing territorial units in order to promote sport activities.

§2. The Employer/Employee Relationship in Czech Law

93. The employment relationship in Czech law is regulated especially, but not exclusively, by the Labour Code.[89] The rights and obligations between the respective two subjects of the employment relationship – the employer and the employee – are regulated in the *labour contract.* The labour contract is the predominant and decisive legal act that establishes the employment.[90] It is a bilateral legal act consisting of a mutual expression of will of the employee and the employer to enter into an employment relationship. The written form is obligatory while stipulating the labour contracts.

87. Former Czechoslovak Socialist Republic.
88. *See* Act No. 115/2001 Coll., on support of sport, as amended.
89. *See* Act No. 262/2006 Coll., the Labour Code, as amended.
90. *See* Bělina, M., Drápal, L. a kol.: Zákoník práce. Komentář. (The Labour Code. Commentary.) 2. Edition, Praha, C. H. Beck, 2015.

The basic source of the labour law is in the Czech Republic the above-mentioned Labour Code. The Labour Code in connection with the Civil Code (which is used subsidiary in case the Labour Code does not rule this off and simultaneously does not regulate the particular situation), governs legal relationships arising from the performance of the dependent work between employees and the employer, whereas these relationships are labour law relationships.

94. The essential difference between the labour and the civil (and possibly commercial) law consist in public law interventions into the contractual relationships within the labour law, which significantly reduce the contractual freedom. This was the main principle of the nineteenth century protection law, when the state provided protection to the economically weaker side of the contractual relationship, i.e. the employee, and such basic principle remains characteristic for the labour law also in the twenty-first century. Public interventions significantly reduce the contractual freedom between the parties, i.e. between employers and employees. In addition, the individual contractual freedom is within the framework of the labour law also limited by the expression of the collective will, i.e. the collective agreement. This is the fundamental difference from the private legal regulation. In particular, the labour law of the Czech Republic has been significantly affected by the law of the European Communities since the end of the 1990s.[91] Before the accession of the Czech Republic to the EU, the process of harmonization has already started and, after joining the EU, the implementation process is continuing, bringing further interventions into the Czech labour law in connection with the European Community law.

The fundamental characteristic of the labour contracts, unlike other private law agreements, is the fact that labour contracts stipulate the dependent work. The labour contract creates the relationship of superiority and subordination between the respective contracting parties. The employer is authorized to give instructions to his employees and the employee is required to respect such instructions. The legal framework for labour contracts then reflects the crucial dominant status of the employer.

95. In the Czech law with regard to contracts in general it is distinguished between the substantive requirements[92] and other requirements to be included within the contract. The substantive requirements of the labour contract are the following:[93]

- the stipulated type of work (job title) which the employee will perform for the employer;
- the place or places of work where the stipulated type of work will be performed by the employee;
- the date of commencement of employment (i.e. of the employment relationship).

The other usual requirements of the labour contract are the following:

- the term of employment – may be stipulated as fixed or indefinite;
- the length of trial period;

91. That is, the process of harmonization of the Czech labour law with the laws of EU took place before Czech Republic became the member state of the EU in 2004.
92. *See* §§ 1732 et seq. of the Act No. 89/2012 Coll., the Civil Code, as amended.
93. *See* § 34 s. 1 of Act No. 262/2006 Coll., the Labour Code, as amended.

- the entitlement to the duration of the vacation provided by the employer – the basic time is four weeks, but may be increased by the employer;
- the amount of wage and the due date, the manner of payment of the wage;
- the scheduling of the working hours and its layout, etc.

It is necessary to note that the standard adjustment of the Labour Code is particularly suitable for the standard labour relationship, i.e. the working hours as of 40 hours a week, where the working time is spread evenly over five working days as of 8 hours a day.

96. With regard to the above described general labour law it is therefore obvious that certain specifics of the sporting activities – for example the matches being played in a viewer's top time (weekends or evenings), the multistage training, the sports camps, the obligation of the athlete to maintain healthy life and refrain from dangerous activities, etc., may be considered as being classified according to the 'classical employment relationship' for the typical employees only with great difficulties. For this reason, it is only possible to recommend that in the event that the regulation of the relationship between the athlete and the club would be subject to the amendment of the Labour Code, the legislator should modify the specifics of sporting activities as outlined above in the form of a possible deviation from the general rules of labour law.

§3. Legal Status of Players and Athletes

97. In general, it may be stated that, within the framework of activities of the professional athletes and players we may find the principles of the so-called *dependent* work as defined within the Czech labour law.[94] However, the extent of dependence in the relationship between the professional athlete (mostly football player and ice hockey player) and his club remains a question extensively discussed in theory and subject to several decisions of courts in the Czech Republic. The *dependent work* is the concept of labour law where between the employee and the employer, in our case between the professional athlete and the club to which the athlete is contractually bound, may be seen signs of employer superiority and the subordination of the employee, the club determines when and where the player shall be present at the training session or competition, the player is obliged to follow the club's instructions and internal regulations, for his activity the player is paid by the club and the club also pays all the associated costs. The player is thus undoubtedly active at the time determined by the club and at the determined place.

98. Being active in a collective sport, the player unconditionally needs the cooperation of the club and the other teammates. In such a case, it is possible to argue whether the performance of collective sport fulfils one of the definition character of trade and thus independence. The player in a collective sport performs on behalf of the club and typically has a number of duties that result from his/her relationship with

94. The main sources of the Czech labour law are three acts: Act No. 262/2006 Coll., the Labour Code, as amended, Act No. 2/1991 Coll., on collective bargaining, as amended and Act No. 435/2004 Coll., on employment, as amended.

the club. As mentioned before, the fact that the player is being a part of a sports team, may (within the relationship between the athlete and the club) hint at the elements of the dependent work as defined by the Labour Code. These duties containing elements of the dependency may be summarized as:

- the obligation to participate in matches, training and camps according to the club's instructions;
- the obligation to maintain physical performance and lifestyle as instructed by the club,
- the obligation not to engage in prohibited sporting activities without the consent of the club;
- the obligation to undergo treatments and rehabilitation as instructed by the club.

99. Furthermore, the player must typically meet a number of other conditions and restrictions that are not applicable in the area of 'common' labour law – the players may be forbidden to carry out certain 'risky' activities (skiing, mountaineering, etc.), they are usually obliged to meet particular diet criteria and may be fined for breach of their health regimen (i.e. in case of an excessive weight gain). The player is thus forced to comply with a number of limitations that cannot be imagined in a standard employment relationship. Additionally, the time when the athlete provides his services to the club differs distinctively from the working hours of the typical employee according to the Czech labour law.

100. As a result of the mentioned absence of the special legal regulation of the status of the professional athletes in the Czech law, the total majority of professional athletes (players) and clubs in collective sports have historically worked with the legal status of the player as the self-employed person (an entrepreneur) providing his services to the club on the basis of a commercial legal arrangement of the so-called professional contract. This legal status of the player as the self-employed person has been preferred by both the clubs and the players over the employer/employee relationship ever since the change of political regime in 1989 because from the tax and social security point of view it saved expenses to both sides of the contractual relationship. However, the legal status of players in collective sports as football and ice hockey, who have been earning above-average wages while also enjoying the tax advantageous status of self-employed persons, has been repeatedly criticized and the discussions within the general public about the extent of the dependent work and other characteristics of employment in the relationship between the player and the club never stopped.

101. Consequently, in relation to the legal status of players we may consider as crucial one of the decisions of the Supreme Administrative Court of the Czech Republic,[95] which stated *that the activity of a professional athlete is not simply subordinate to the concept of dependent work within the meaning of Section 2 (3) of the Labour Code of 2006.*[96] *It is therefore not unlawful to conclude contracts other than labour contracts between athletes and their respective clubs. From the tax point of view, an athlete can*

95. *See* the decision of the Supreme Administrative Court of Czech Republic dated 29 Nov. 2011, file number 2 Afs 16 / 2011-78, [2510/2012 Coll. NSS].

96. This statement is interpreted as meaning that the relationship between the athlete and the club cannot be considered as the usual or typical employment relationship.

also act as a self-employed person. Accordingly, it can be concluded from this respective decision that the activity of a professional athlete is not automatically subordinate to the concept of dependent employment within the meaning of the labour law and the stipulation of other types of contracts defining the relationship between athletes (players) and clubs must be considered as in compliance with the Czech law. This legal assumption is currently accepted despite the updated wording of the Labour Code,[97] where dependent work is defined as *work that is carried out within the relationship of the employer's superiority and his employee's subordination in the employer's name and according to the employer's instructions (orders) and that is performed in person by the employee for his employer.*

102. To summarize, the legal status of the professional athlete (player) is not stipulated in the Czech law neither by a special act, nor does any special legal regulation refer to the specifics of sport activities and athletes' relationship with clubs. It can be repeatedly mentioned that the athletes currently have no special legal status in the Czech Republic, but the mutual rights and obligations of the athletes and respective clubs are governed by the regular legislation, using certain specifics necessary and needed for the proper performance of sports activities. With respect to the aforementioned decision of the Supreme Administrative Court, the choice of the manner of legal regulation in order to establish their mutual legal relationship is on the selection of the respective contractual parties (i.e. the athlete and the club), whereas the parties may use the following forms:

- the employer/employee relationship pursuant to the Labour Code[98] or;
- the contractual relationship pursuant to the Civil Code, when the contract between the athlete (player) and the club is typically stipulated pursuant to the provision of § 1746 of the Civil Code (as the so-called unnamed agreement), i.e. contract is not specified in the Civil Code or other law as a special contract type, typically just contract of the performance of sporting activities. While stipulating such contract, the general limits of autonomy of contractual parties shall apply, i.e. it is not possible to conclude the contract that would limit basic human rights, such as a slavery agreement. However, the specific scope and content of the mutual rights and obligations of the athlete and the club is determined in accordance with the mutual 'business' agreement of the parties.

103. However, it is important to say that the pressure from UEFA and FIFPro on the European national football associations[99] has led to the fact that in majority of European countries the football players enter into employer/employee relationships with professional clubs. As the Czech Republic is one of the few remaining countries where the football players do not have the status of employees, but instead enter into private contracts with Czech football clubs, it is sensible to predict that this change of status of football players is inevitable and only a matter of time. It is obvious that this

97. *See* § 2 of the Act No. 262/2006 Coll., Labour Code, as amended.
98. In reality this almost never happens.
99. A working group with representatives from UEFA, FIFPro, EPFL, ECA and European Commission has been established to discuss steps that will be taken to ensure this unification of the status of football players in Europe.

change will require changes in the current legislation, either by updating the Labour Code or by issuing a new sports act, which may acknowledge the specific status of athletes (players) in collective sports as a special type of employer/employee relationship with its own specific rules and specific tax aspects.

104. The activity of the professional athlete in the individual sport can be classified under the Trades Licensing Act, because the trade is legally defined as a continuous activity operated independently, on his own behalf, on his own responsibility, in order to obtain profit and under the conditions stipulated by the law,[100] whereas the sport activity is not mentioned in the negative definition of the trade according to the provisions of Section 3 of the Trade Licensing Act. Within the framework of the so-called free trade, we can find the subject *operation of sports and sports facilities and the organization of sporting activities*[101], where, according to the relevant governmental regulation,[102] the activity of the high-performing athletes is also included.

105. Last but not least, it is necessary to realize that it is usually not enough for the sports activity just to conclude a contract between the athlete and the club, but it is also necessary to register such a contract by the respective association. The registration of the contract is usually the necessary condition of the eligibility of the player. In addition to the requirement to register a contract, there may be other limitations, for the proper exercise of sporting activities like for example the need to obtain a special licence (FIA[103] car races, etc.).

§4. Fundamental Rights and Obligations for Clubs and Players

106. It can be stated that the basic rights and duties of the clubs and players are derived from the content of the logic of the sport performance of the respective sporting activity. The Football Association of Czech Republic is using a model league professional contract,[104] that is in practice used by most of the professional clubs of the first and second league without any important changes. With its scope of rights and obligations of contracting parties and covered areas it is without a doubt the most complex contract being stipulated between the athlete and the club in a collective sport in the Czech Republic. When taken into consideration ice hockey, in the Czech Republic similarly popular as football, the Czech Ice Hockey Federation (CSLH) uses a model obligatory contract[105] between the player and the club with the rights and conditions of the

100. *See* § 2 of the Act No. 455/1991 Coll., the Trade Licensing Act, as amended.
101. *See* the Amendment No. 4 to the Act. No. 455/1991 Coll., the Trade Licensing Act, as amended.
102. *See* the governmental Regulation No. 278/2008 Coll., on establishing the content of the trade licences, which classifies the activities of high-performing athletes under the activity No. 74 of the unrestricted trade as defined in the Trade Licensing Act.
103. *See* the official website of the International Automobile Federation (Federation Internationale de l'Automobile): https://www.fia.com/.
104. The 'league professional contract' is a type of professional contract which is according to the Regulations of FACR being used by professional clubs of the first and second league. Non-professional clubs use the 'standard professional contract', which in comparison to the league professional contract is simpler.
105. *See* the model contract between the player and the club on the official website of the Czech Ice Hockey Federation (CSLH): www.cslh.cz.

contracting parties vaguely similar but defined in a more simpler way. This contract is obligatory for both contracting parties and the rights and obligations of the parties are predefined. Therefore, the parties only agree the wage of the player and the duration of the contract and after signing, the contract is ready to be registered.

107. The model league professional contract[106] of FACR complies with the Transfer Regulations[107] of FACR, which determine: (i) *the general requirements* of the professional contract (identification of contracting parties including their legal guardians and intermediaries representing the parties, type of the professional contract (league or standard), specific identification number within the FACR informational system, etc.), (ii) *the minimum obligations of the player* (other obligations may be added based on the negotiation of the parties), (iii) *the minimum obligations of the club* (other obligations may be added based on the negotiation of the parties), (iv) *various obligations have to be included in the contract binding both contracting parties, to be stipulated to a certain degree according to the negotiation of the parties* (the notice period in case of termination of the contract for a specific reason has to be stipulated but its length is up to parties, the percentage of automatic decrease of the remuneration paid to the player in case of the relegation of the club has to be stipulated, but the actual percentage is up to the negotiation of the parties) and finally (iv) *the prohibited stipulations that may not be included in the professional contract* (the precedent condition in the form of the player receiving the work permit in Czech Republic, the precedent condition in the form of the player passing a medical examination to a satisfaction of the club).

108. It is obvious that the core of the professional contract is determined by the Transfer Regulations of FACR and the parties are able to modify this professional contract only to a certain extent as further modification in breach of the Transfer Regulations of FACR would lead to such professional contract not being registered by FACR and thus to the player's ineligibility in competitive matches played by the club. The essential requirements while stipulating the professional contract are: (i) the contract has to comply with law[108] and good morals and (ii) the written form. The professional contract may be stipulated in minimum until the end of the current season, in maximum for five years (maximum of three years in case of the player younger than 18 years). The clubs are allowed to sign professional contracts with players who are at least 15 years old.

106. Both model professional contracts (league and standard) prepared by FACR are available at the official board of FACR accessible through the official website of FACR: www.fotbal.cz.

107. *See* §§ 18 et seq. of the Transfer Regulations of the Football Association of Czech Republic, effective as of 1 Jul. 2017, available at the official website of FACR: (www.fotbal.cz), https://facr.fotbal.cz/uredni-deska-predpisy/193?category=1.

108. In general, all contracts stipulating mutual rights and obligations between an athlete and a club (in sports that do not use model contracts approved by the relevant national association) must fulfil all legal requirements; in the theoretical case of a labour agreement, the form and content of the contract must comply with the Labour Code and, in the case of other contractual arrangements with the Civil Code. Failure to comply with statutory requirements may lead to the invalid agreement.

109. The minimum player's obligations required by the Transfer Regulations of FACR to be included in the league professional contract may be summarized as the following:

- The obligations to perform *the primary duties of a football player*, i.e. to his best ability participate in training sessions, training camps, prematch preparations, and to carry out individual training according to the club's instructions and to participate in matches the player is selected for regardless of whether the match in question is a part of a league, cup, tournament or a friendly.
- Apart from participating in trainings and matches the player is at all times obliged *to care for his health and fitness level*, comply with the principles of daily routine of a professional athlete, correct nutrition and regime, hygiene, regeneration and rehabilitation, submit to all established treatment procedures and avoid the use of doping in any form.
- *Representing the club outside of the pitch* is becoming more and more important, the player is contractually obliged to participate in various social events and in media to promote the sponsors of the club and the image and goodwill of the club.
- The player is contractually obliged to *use training equipment and clothing provided by the club sponsors*, this often includes football shoes.
- To make maximum efforts to achieve *the sporting objectives of the club*, compete in the matches fairly, to know and comply with the rules of FACR, FIFA and UEFA and orders of the club and to take care to avoid damages to health of both the player and of his fellow players and competitors.
- The player is furthermore obliged *to comply with the club's rules and administrative and internal regulations* (club's Disciplinary Code, club's code of conduct, etc.) and with the decisions of the club's coaching staff and management, and to maintain confidentiality with regard to the internal affairs and processes of the club; however , the player is entitled, in the attendance of the captain of the team, in which he currently performs the sporting activity, to express his disagreement with the disciplinary decision of the club towards the player; the club undertakes to discuss such disagreement with the player.[109]
- Specific obligations are stipulated with regard to *the health care of the player*. The player should inform the club without delay in case of a disease or accident and not to undergo, with the exception of emergency cases, any medical treatments without a prior provision of information to the club doctor. On the contrary, the player is obliged to undergo, at the request of the club doctor, regular medical examinations and medical treatments.
- The player cannot, during the contract period, participate in other sports or dangerous activities unless the club has approved the activities in writing.
- A special emphasis is put on *refraining from certain activities* involving betting, games and competitions connected with the matches of the club.
- The player is obliged to comply with the relevant accounting and tax regulations, to issue invoices to enable the club to provide him with stipulated payments on

109. This stipulation does not oblige the club to revise its disciplinary measure in anyway, it merely ensures that the player's opinion is heard by the club management.

time and to *pay taxes, social security and health insurance* according to the valid applicable laws.[110]

- The player is also obliged to inform the club about any disciplinary sanctions imposed on him before his transfer to the club otherwise he has to cover the damages of the club caused to the clubs by this (i.e. for example the fine for fielding an ineligible player).

110. On the other hand , the club's obligations arising from the Transfer Regulations of FACR may be summarized in the following ways:

- *The payment obligations of the club towards the player* – to pay the player properly and timely monthly[111] wages and other bonuses as agreed (e.g., for games played, for goals scored, etc.), it is explicitly stated that the monthly wage is due even in case the player is injured and cannot play.
- The obligation to create for players the *adequate conditions* for successful pursuit of sports activities mainly during matches and training (including food and transportation), to ensure quality medical, regeneration, rehabilitation and therapeutic service.
- The club is also obliged to provide the player with *regular medical examinations* while maintaining the complete medical documentation of the player, including health complications arising during the performance of the obligations in the national team, in cooperation with the club medical staff. The club is also obliged to enable the player to request, at his own costs, an opinion of an independent medical expert in case he has objections to the opinion of the club medical staff.
- The obligation to provide the player with at least one day off in a calendar week; on condition that the frequency of training or matches or other serious reasons do not enable the provision of such rest, the club is obliged to enable the player to draw such rest in accumulation in the nearest possible period usually in the middle of and at the end of the season; to provide paid rest within the range of four weeks per each period of twelve months, and within the said period of rest, a continuous period of fourteen consecutive calendar days shall be provided within the calendar year without reducing the monthly remuneration in compliance with the approved plan of the sport preparation; the continuous period of rest may be used, after an agreement of the player and the club even by parts, in all

---

110. It is interesting that even though this is not the obligation of a player towards the club, but more like a general obligation of the player towards the authorities arising from the fact that he is economically active in the country, it has still been incorporated in the Transfer Regulations of FACR based on the historical experience of clubs, that the player pursued by authorities on usually also debt collectors for not paying his taxes is usually not able to focus properly on training and matches and is not able to provide the club with his services as expected.
111. The minimum monthly wage in case of the league professional contract is CZK 10,000 (approximately EUR 400), in case of the standard professional contract CZK 5,000 (approximately EUR 200).

cases the day of the beginning of the continuous period of rest shall be established by the club;[112]

- With a prior consent of the coach the club is also obliged to provide the player with additional free time to enable him to arrange his private matters without reducing the payments towards the player.
- In case of the youth players the club is obliged to enable them to participate in regular studies without reducing their monthly remuneration.

According to the Transfer Regulations the club and the player are also both obliged to include additional stipulations in the league professional contract, for example the negotiated use of the personality rights of the player by the club or the percentage of the automatic decrease of the player's wages according to the professional contract in case the club is relegated.[113]

111. To summarize the above described, within certain national sport associations the so-called *agreement evidence* is being used. The principle of such evidence is that the relevant sports association determines in its internal legal regulations:

- the content of the contract between the club and the player and/or its binding draft;
- the obligation to register the contract between the club and the player whereas only registered contracts can lead to the respective rights and obligations of the parties being enforceable in the proceedings within the respective association.[114]

Such a procedure can be considered as suitable from a practical point of view because, upon the absence of specific legal regulation in the area of sport, such internal legal regulations stipulating the content of the contract may prove very practical from both the point of view of athletes and clubs.

112. In practice this stipulation is often not fully complied with as especially during the first part of the season the clubs often participate in several competitions (first league, FACR Cup, Europa League) and while the players are also being called to the national teams, it is difficult to find a day off during the crammed training schedules. As for the cumulative vacation, one part is usually provided in December during the winter break of the league competition and second one in the first half of June, before the start of the preparation for the next season which usually starts in the second half of July depending mostly on the access of the clubs into the qualification rounds of the UEFA Europa League and UEFA Champions League, which take place before the start of the league competition at the end of July.

113. As this stipulation is obligatory and has to be part of the professional contract, but the percentage of the decrease is up to the negotiations between the club and the player, in practice the percentage almost shockingly varies between 50% and 5%.

114. As a typical example of this practice, we can mention the Registration Regulations of FACR (available at https://facr.fotbal.cz/uredni-deska-predpisy/192?category=1) or the Registration Regulations of the Czech Ice Hockey Federation (CSLH) (available at http://www.cslh.cz/text/121-stanovy-a-rady.html).

§5. Agents Regulation

I. General Issues

112. A sports agent is generally the entity mediating on behalf of the player (athlete) the negotiations concerning his contract with clubs, furthermore mediates two clubs' negotiations with a goal of concluding a player transfer agreement or negotiates the terms of contracts for the use of the marketing potential of the athlete.

The typical activities of agent in sport are:

- the providing of various legal, accounting or investment services to the athlete;
- the providing of a trainer services, nutrition adviser, physiotherapist and other health care, mental coach to the athlete and basically any services to help enhance the athlete's performance;
- the providing of the personal administration for the athlete;
- the providing of personal assistance (finding housing, schools for children, etc.) for athlete.

Within the individual sports, the subject of the agent's activity is primarily to find sponsors to pay for the marketing activities of the athlete. Furthermore, within the collective sports, apart from fulfilling the marketing potential of the player (athlete), the key role of the agent working for the respective player is to secure a new agreement and/or to ensure transfer or loan of the player to another club. Therefore, the role of the player's agent in collective sport has a huge impact on the player's career in its entirety. In football negotiating the right transfer of the talented player to a right club at the right phase of the player's career, thus enabling him to further develop his talent, may become the key factor in determining the overall success of the player's career. Sadly, the opposite is also true, the wrong transfer or loan may slow down the promisingly developing player usually keeping him off the pitch and within his by estimate fifteen-year long professional career also costing him precious time to get back into the playing shape and his career back on track.

113. The agent usually acts for a fee and the relationship between the agent and the player is established on the basis of a contract. The agent can act as an individual (natural person) or as a corporation (legal person). The agents, of course, must comply with all generally binding legal regulations while performing their activities. The key issue for the agent's activity is whether or not the respective national sports association regulates the activities of agents or not. If the activity is not regulated, the content of the mutual rights and obligations is based on the agreement between the agent and the player. It is then entirely up to them (as the contracting parties) what type of contract shall be concluded and how shall the mutual rights and obligations between the athlete and the agent be stipulated (of course within the framework of the generally binding legal regulations).

II. Registered Intermediaries in Football

114. In some sports, however, the agents' activities are strictly regulated. One of the sports that historically strictly regulates the activities of the agents (in the present day called the registered intermediaries) is football. The Football Association of the Czech Republic, as the national sports association in charge of football within the Czech Republic and the membership organization of UEFA and FIFA, regulates the activities of intermediaries in compliance with the FIFA Regulations on Working with Intermediaries,[115] which serve as the minimum requirements to be implemented on the national level.[116] However, this system adopted in 2015 enabled the national associations to create their own rules and inevitably led to establishing of various subsystems with different rules and conditions for conduct of the intermediary activity. The Czech Republic is no exception, since the adoption of the new rules it has been much more difficult for professional clubs to work with foreign intermediaries, ergo signing of foreign players has become administratively more difficult. The most obvious shortcoming of the Czech Intermediary Regulations is, however, also the most obvious one, as one of the rules created by FACR is even in direct contradiction with the FIFA Regulations on Working with Intermediaries, allowing the Czech registered intermediaries to receive payments from players and clubs for transfers of minors (or negotiating professional contracts) older than sixteen years.[117] The FIFA Regulations on Working with Intermediaries in fact clearly state[118] that the players and clubs that engage the services of an intermediary when negotiating an employment contract and/or transfer agreement are prohibited from making any payments to such intermediary if the player concerned is a minor, as defined in point 11 of the Definitions section of the Regulations on the Status and Transfer of Players[119] (there the minor is defined as a player who has not yet reached the age of 18).

115. The basic document for the regulation of the activities of the registered intermediaries are the FACR Statutes,[120] as well as the Intermediary Regulations.[121] The Intermediary Regulations stipulate the basic rules regarding the relations between FACR, the intermediaries, the players and the clubs, in relation to the intermediary activities. The Intermediation Regulations determine both the conditions of registering

115. *See* FIFA Regulations on working with Intermediaries, available at the official website of FIFA: (www.fifa.com), https://www.fifa.com/mm/document/affederation/administration/02/36/77/63/regulationsonworkingwithintermediariesii_neutral.pdf.

116. *See* Colucci, Michele (ed.), *The FIFA Regulations on Working with Intermediaries. Its Implementation on National Level*, Sports Law and Policy Centre, 2015, segment Czech Republic (country report) by Martin Procházka, pp. 251 et seq.

117. *See* § 9 Art. 7 of the Intermediary Regulations at the official website of FACR: (www.fotbal.cz), https://facr.fotbal.cz/uredni-deska-predpisy/197?category=1.

118. *See* the Art. 7 s. 8 of FIFA Regulations on working with Intermediaries, available at the official website of FIFA: www.fifa.com.

119. *See* FIFA Regulations on Status and Transfer of Players, available at the official website of FIFA: www.fifa.com.

120. *See* the Art. 16 and following of the Statutes of FACR, available at the official website of FACR: www.fotbal.cz.

121. *See* the FACR Intermediary Regulations, available on the official website of FACR: www.fotbal.cz.

as the intermediary in Czech Republic and further the basic mutual rights and obligations of intermediaries, clubs and players. The Intermediary Regulations also determine[122] in particular the content and form of the representation contract stipulated between intermediaries on one side and the players or clubs, on the other side.

The representation contract must be stipulated in writing before the intermediary commences the intermediary activity and must have the following content:

- the precise identification of the contracting parties;
- the specification of the contractual relationship;
- the remuneration of the intermediary and the payment terms;
- the clause whether the respective contract is concluded as an exclusive or non-exclusive;
- the time period for which the contract concluded, indicating the agreed start and end of the intermediary activity; the conditions for the premature termination of the contract; the date of the stipulation of the contract;
- a valid arbitration clause, on the basis of which the disputes will be settled in accordance with the FACR Statutes and the internal regulations of the FACR published on the basis thereof;
- signatures of all contracting parties.

The representation contract may be concluded for a maximum of three years and may not be concluded with a player who is not yet 15 years old. If a player is younger than 18 years old,[123] the representation contract must be signed by his/her legal representative.[124]

The representation contract shall be drawn up in at least two copies, each party shall receive at least one copy. A one copy of each representation contract between the intermediary and the player must be inserted into the Electronic Information System of the FACR, provided only in the Czech or Slovak language. If the representation contract is concluded in another language, it can be inserted into the Electronic Information System of the FACR only as an officially certified translation into the Czech language. This insertion into the system of the FACR ensures that the content of the respective contracts complies with all the mandatory requirements of FACR legislation and regulations.

116. The activities of agents in football are supervised by a special body, namely the commission for the activities of agents appointed by the Executive Committee of FACR. As of 7 September 2017, more than eighty intermediaries (both legal and natural persons) were registered at FACR.[125] Every year FACR releases the separate total amounts paid to registered intermediaries by players and by clubs. In 2016, the total amount paid to FACR registered intermediaries by players was CZK 1,085,115.[126] In

---

122. *See* §§ 7 et seq. of the FACR Intermediary Regulations at the official website of FACR: www.fotbal.cz.
123. For the legal definition of a minor see § 30 of the Civil Code.
124. Usually the parents of the minor – see § 829 and following of the Civil Code.
125. The list of the registered intermediaries is available at the official website of FACR: www.fotbal.cz.
126. Published in accordance with Art. 6 s. 3 of the FIFA Regulations on working with Intermediaries.

comparison the amount paid by Czech clubs to registered intermediaries was more than CZK 100 million.[127]

III. Intermediaries (Agents) in Ice Hockey

117. The Czech Ice Hockey Federation (CSLH) chose a different approach in the area of the regulation of agents' activities. CSLH offers an intermediary certificate with the official title 'Players' intermediary (agent) registered at CSLH', which confirms that the intermediary has fulfilled certain conditions, in particular: (i) signing the request for the intermediary certificate while providing information about the intermediary, (ii) providing CSLH with the excerpt from the commercial register in case of a legal person or the excerpt from the trade register in case of a natural person, (iii) signing the Codex of the intermediary,[128] (iv) signing the declaration regarding the clean criminal record of the intermediary or his/her cooperating persons and (v) paying a registration fee. After fulfilling these conditions, the legal or natural person is granted the certificate by the Executive Committee of CSLH, this certificate being of a certain information value to the players and especially to the parents of young players about the conduct of the intermediary in general. However, the lack of the certificate does not prevent anyone from performing intermediary activities or working as a players' agent in Czech ice hockey. The difference between the rules in hockey and football is obvious, while the intermediary activities in Czech hockey are in reality not regulated as the certificate is only optional, in football the registration of the intermediary is a necessary and obligatory condition to perform any intermediary activity in Czech football.

§6. The Settlement of Disputes

118. As a general rule which applies in the Czech law, the disputes and other legal matters arising from private law matters are decided by the general courts of the Czech Republic. Similarly, the courts in the administrative judiciary with the Supreme Administrative Court as the supreme body decide in general the disputes regarding the decisions in the area of public administration. The question of the jurisdiction (both local and substantive) as well as the system of courts is then determined pursuant to the relevant procedural rules.[129]

119. In the case of property disputes, the arbitration tribunal may, in general, be the place where the dispute is decided in accordance with the Czech laws on arbitration,[130] in such case the decision of the arbitration tribunal replaces the decision

127. Approximately EUR 4,000,000.

128. The Codex of the intermediary contains several rules regarding the suitable conduct of intermediaries and is available at the official website of CSLH: (www.cslh.cz), http://www.cslh.cz/agenti-kodex.html.

129. *See* Act No. 99/1963 Coll., the code of civil procedure, as amended.

130. *See* Act No. 216/1994 Coll., on arbitration proceedings and on execution of arbitral awards, as amended.

of the court.[131] The function of an arbitrator may arise on an *ad hoc basis* where the arbitrator may generally be a citizen of the Czech Republic who is of legal age, has a clean criminal register and legal capability, or the case may be entrusted to the decision of the permanent arbitral tribunal. The most well-known and well-respected permanent arbitration tribunal in the Czech Republic is the Arbitration Court attached to the Economic Chamber of the Czech Republic and the Agricultural Chamber of the Czech Republic[132] established in 1949.[133] In any case, for the dispute between two parties to be settled by arbitration, both parties have to agree with the arbitration. It can therefore be stated that, unless there is a specific stipulation between the parties, all disputes in the field of sport are typically decided by general courts.

120. The general courts further resolve disputes arising between the parties arising from the employment relationship based on the labour contract. With regard to the procedural rules of the Czech Republic, it can be stated that in case of the labour contract concluded between the club and the player (even though this is rather hypothetical because this in practice does not happen), any disputes between its parties, that is, the employee and the employer, are decided by the general courts.

121. A slightly different situation may arise in the case that the relationship between the player and the club is not based on a labour contract but on the private contract, which happens in absolute majority of cases. In such case, according to the internal regulations of the particular national sports association, it is first necessary to decide the dispute within the arbitration bodies of the respective national sports association. For some national sports associations, typically FACR (football) and CSLH (ice hockey), the situation is such that, on the contrary, every intervention of the court in the jurisdiction of arbitration bodies is perceived to be very problematic. The same applies in case of the dispute about the proper performance of sporting activities (adherence to the rules), where such disputes are more expertly decided in the course of the internal disciplinary proceedings of the relevant national sports association.

122. If we consider the rules of the Football Association of Czech Republic as an example, then, under its regulations, the General Assembly is the supreme authority of FACR. The statutory body of FACR is the Executive Committee of FACR, FACR is able to act legally either by the Chairman and one of the Vice-Chairmen of the Executive Committee together or by two Vice-Chairs of the Executive Committee

131. For more on this see Raban, Přemysl: Alternativní řešení sporů, arbitráž a rozhodci v České a Slovenské Republice a zahraničí (The Alternative Dispute Resolution, the Arbitration and Arbitrators in Czech and Slovak Republic and Abroad), C. H. Beck, Praha, 2004, pp. 75 et seq., pp. 144 et seq.

132. For more information about the agenda of the Arbitration Court attached to the Economic Chamber of Czech Republic and the Agricultural Chamber of the Czech Republic see the official website: http://en.soud.cz/.

133. *See* Růžička, Květoslav: Rozhodčí řízení před Rozhodčím soudem při Hospodářské komoře České republiky a Agrární komoře České republiky (The Arbitration Proceedings at the Arbitration Court Attached to the Economic Chamber of Czech Republic and the Agricultural Chamber of the Czech Republic), Aleš Čeněk, Pelhřimov, 2003, pp. 55 et seq.

together. The first respective body of FACR, elected by the General Assembly, dealing with disputes within FACR is the Board of Appeal.[134]

123. The Board of Appeal of FACR has seven members elected by the General Assembly of FACR for four years. The Chairman and the Vice-Chairman of the Board of Appeal are elected by the other members of the Board of Appeal. According to the Statutes of FACR the member of the Board of Appeal may not be a member of any other elected body of FACR including being active as a delegate or referee in football competitions from certain level precisely determined by the Statutes of FACR, to establish the independence of the members of the Board of Appeals. The decisions and the activity of the Board of Appeal is independent of the other bodies of FACR. The Board of Appeal decides mainly in the following matters:

- as the appeal body regarding the disputes connected with FACR membership and the special rights and obligations connected herewith;
- as the second-instance body for the appeals against decisions of the following bodies of FACR:
  - the Ethical Committee of FACR;
  - the Disciplinary Committee of the League Football Association;
  - the Disciplinary Committee of the Steering Committee for Bohemia and the Disciplinary Committee of the Steering Committee for Moravia;
  - the League Committee on Governance and Security of the national league competitions;
  - Sport and Technical Committee of the Steering Committee for Bohemia and Sports and Technical Commission of the Steering Committee for Moravia;
  - as the authority in extraordinary appeals against decisions issued in the appeal proceedings by the bodies of the regional football associations, Prague Football Association and District Football Associations in competitive and disciplinary matters;
  - as the deciding body in case of conflicts of competency between the bodies of FACR, etc.

124. The main body authorized to decide the disputes between the members of FACR, that otherwise would have been decided by the general courts (these are mostly property disputes), is the Board of Arbitrators.[135] The Board of Arbitrators is constituted by the list of arbitrators kept and made public by FACR. The arbitrators are registered by the Executive Committee of FACR from the candidates suggested by member clubs of FACR or players registered at FACR. The number of arbitrators on the list of arbitrators is not limited. The disputes in the arbitration proceedings are decided by: (i) single arbitrator or (ii) the senate of three arbitrators, while the first instance decision may be appealed to the senate of five arbitrators. The arbitrators are chosen from the

134. *See* the Arts 24 et seq. of the Statutes of FACR, available on the official website of FACR: (www.fotbal.cz), https://facr.fotbal.cz/uredni-deska-predpisy/177?category=1.

135. *See* the Arts 26 et seq. of the Statutes of FACR on the official website of FACR: www.fotbal.cz.

above-mentioned list of arbitrators. The following disputes are decided in the arbitration proceedings according to the Procedural Regulations of FACR:

- The disputes arising from the written contracts between:
  - the FACR member clubs and players, if the professional contracts are registered by the FACR;
  - the FACR member clubs and coaches and trainers;
  - the FACR member clubs on issues relating to transfers and loans of players, unless otherwise provided by a regulation issued pursuant to the statutes of FACR;
  - the registered intermediaries and players in case of contracts registered by FACR;
  - the registered intermediaries and clubs in case of contracts registered by FACR.
- The disputes related to severance payments and training compensations.

These proceedings are a two instance arbitration within FACR. Against the final decision decided within FACR it is possible to file an appeal action to CAS[136] or to general courts of Czech Republic. The disciplinary misconducts of the participants of the football matches are then solved by respective disciplinary committees where the procedure is analogous to the proceedings within international structures – the Control, Ethics and Disciplinary Body and the Appeals Body.[137]

§7. Social Security

125. The social security in general is *any government system that provides monetary assistance to people with an inadequate or no income*[138]. The social security system in the Czech Republic includes basic compulsory retirement insurance and the sickness insurance.

I. The Retirement Insurance

126. The participation within the basic retirement insurance system is obligatory subject to the stipulated conditions. There are two basic groups of insured subjects:

136. *See* the official website of the Court of Arbitration for Sport: http://www.tas-cas.org/en/index.html.

137. *See* the official website of UEFA: https://www.uefa.com/insideuefa/disciplinary/disciplinary-cases/index.html.

138. *See* Bach, David, *1001 Financial Words You Need to Know*. Oxford University Press, USA, 2003, p. 185.

(1) the employed persons (including athletes in employment) in labour relationship; and
(2) the self-employed persons, i.e. athletes operating independently and/or under a contractual (non-labour) relationship with the club.

For all groups (participants), the uniform legal regulations apply, i.e. there is no differentiation in the status of an athlete within the pension insurance. After satisfying all the statutory conditions, a legal entitlement to a retirement pension arises. Basic retirement insurance is economically guaranteed by the state, based on the idea that it is not possible for the state to leave retirees without the source of income on which they are usually dependent. The following payments are provided from the basic retirement insurance:

- the retirement payment (including early retirement) where the condition of entitlement is the required insurance period of at least 25 years and reaching the retirement age (age 65);
- the full disability payment, where the condition of entitlement is the existence of a long-term unfavourable state of health corresponding to full disability;
- the partial disability payment;
- the widow's and widower's payments;
- the orphan payments.

II. The Sickness Insurance

127. The sickness insurance scheme is intended for employed persons irrespective of their legal status, which, in cases of the so-called short-term social events (temporary incapacity for work due to illness or accident or quarantine, nursing, pregnancy and maternity, childcare) receive cash sickness insurance benefits. For the purposes of the sickness insurance under the sickness insurance law, the insured person's citizenship is irrelevant. The participation in the insurance system is obligatory for the employees in the employer/employee relationships according to the Labour Code (therefore also for the employed athletes) and remains voluntary for the self-employed persons.

The following benefits are provided from the sickness insurance:

- the sickness payments;
- the financial help during the maternity;
- the nursing payments;
- the equalization allowance in pregnancy and maternity.

The premium rates within the social security system are established by the Act No. 589/1992, on social security premium and contribution on the state's employment policy, as amended.[139] The premium rates thus determined are calculated from the so-called assessment base, which can be very broadly characterized as the sum of the incomes.

§8. Tax Law

I. The Taxes in General

128. The tax is a mandatory (or otherwise) statutory based payment to the budget of the authority (mostly the state) that is entitled to impose it. The relationship between the tax payer and the authority is characteristic by the inequality of its subjects as the tax is imposed as a one-sided obligation without the payer's claim for any reciprocations form the collecting authority. Taxes are paid in certain specific circumstances, for example, at regular intervals or at the change of ownership (pay, sale, gift, or inheritance).[140]

II. The System of Tax Administration in Czech Republic

129. Tax administration in the Czech Republic is carried out by the state through the system of the financial administration. The central body of the system of the Financial Administration is the General Financial Directorate (GFD)[141] established as of 1 January 2013. The head of the General Financial Directorate is the Director General, who is appointed and dismissed by the Minister of Finance. The financial administration bodies in the Czech Republic are the following:

- the Appellate Financial Directorate is the superior authority for all regional Tax Offices;
- specialized Tax Office – and the respective Tax Office for taxpayers designated by law (bank institutions, insurance companies, legal entities with turnover higher than CZK 2,000,000,000);
- Tax Offices – Basic territorial units of financial administration in the Czech Republic.

---

139. The premium rates as of January 2018 are: (i) for employers 25% of the assessment base, of which 2.3% for sickness insurance, 21.5% for retirement insurance, 1.2% for state employment policy; (ii) for employees 6.5% of the assessment bases; (iii) for self-employed persons 29.2% of the assessment base, of which: 28% for retirement insurance, 1.2% for state employment policy (for self-employed persons voluntarily participating in sickness insurance 2.3% of the assessment base); (iv) for voluntary participants 28% of the assessment base; (v) for foreign employees who voluntarily apply for sickness insurance 2.3% of the assessment base.

140. *See* Jánošíková, Petra; Mrkývka, Petr; Tomažič, Ivan: Finanční a daňové právo (Financial and Tax Law), Aleš Čeněk, Plzeň, 2009, Chapter 2, Tax Law, pp. 298 et seq.

141. *See* the Act No. 456/2011 Coll., On the Financial Administration of the Czech Republic, as amended.

III. The General Tax Obligations

130. The general tax obligations of the respective tax payers in the Czech Republic are the following:[142]

(i) *The Income taxes*:[143] With regard to the personal income tax the taxable period is a calendar year. The personal income tax is payable within three months after the end of the taxable period. In the case of a taxpayer who has the statutory obligation to have the financial statements certified by an auditor or whose tax return is processed by the tax advisor, the tax return is filed six months after the end of the tax period at the latest. The tax return for personal income tax is filed with the tax office – the territorial office of the respective taxpayer. The tax rate is 15% of the income.

With regard to the corporate income tax the taxable period is generally a calendar year or a business year, which shall start on the first day of a month other than January and run for the following twelve successive months. Legal persons with their registered office or place of management in the territory of the Czech Republic are subject to tax liability, which is related to income resulting from both resources in the Czech Republic and resources abroad. Legal persons having neither registered office nor place of management in the Czech Republic are subject to tax liability relating only to income from resources in the territory of the Czech Republic. The tax rate is 19% of the income.

(ii) *The value added tax*[144] *(VAT)*: The VAT is a type of general consumption tax that is collected incrementally, based on the increase in value of a product or service at each stage of its production or distribution. The amount of VAT is determined by the state as a percentage of the end market price. As its name suggests, the value added tax is designed to tax only the value added by a business on top of the services and goods it can purchase from the market. The taxing period is a calendar quarter or (in the case of larger payers i.e. a turnover in excess of CZK 10,000,000) a calendar month. The basic VAT rate is 21%. Additionally, two VAT rates are reduced: (i) 15% (heat, accommodation, catering and drinks); and (ii) 10% (infant food and baby food, medicines, etc.). The Czech tax system also includes: (iii) the real estate tax, (iv) the inheritance tax, the gift tax, the real estate transfer tax, (v) the road tax, (vi) the consumption taxes, (vii) the energy taxes.

IV. The Taxes and Sport

131. From the perspective of the area of sport, the subjects of taxes in the Czech Republic may be: (i) the legal persons – clubs, sports organizations, national sports associations and (ii) the natural persons – athletes (players). As mentioned above, the vast majority of athletes (players) in the Czech Republic have the self-employed status, with the exception of those who are employed in one of the three department sports centres established by the ministries (the University Sport Centre, the Army Sport Centre DUKLA and the OLYMP Sport Centre). Even the players in collective sports

142. For more about taxes in EU countries and interesting comparison in their tax law see the official website of the Confédération Fiscale Européenne: www.cfe-eutax.org.
143. *See* Act No. 586/1992 Coll., on income taxes, as amended.
144. *See* Act No. 235/2004 Coll., on value added tax, as amended.

(i.e. football, ice hockey, etc.) stipulate private agreements with the clubs they play for instead of employment contracts, which gives them the status of the self-employed person. With regard to the income tax most of the athletes therefore keep using the expenses flat rate of 60% in their tax returns[145] as opposed to only 40% expenses flat rate which should be used in case of the so-called independent professions (for example artists).[146] This practice was challenged in recent years by the tax offices by imposing additional taxation on the famous Czech football player David Lafata while arguing that he was obliged to use the 40% expenses flat rate instead of the 60% expenses flat rate, thus questioning the athlete's status as the self-employed person. The case was closely followed by the general public as the athlete challenged the decision of the tax office at court, arguing that as a self-employed person he was entitled by law to use the higher costs flat rate. In the end the Supreme Administrative Court of Czech Republic decided that the player was right to use the higher 60% expenses flat rate, thus confirming the legal and tax status of professional athletes using the trade licence according to the Trade Licensing Act[147] in Czech Republic as self-employed persons.[148] The Supreme Administrative Court of Czech Republic explicitly mentioned the principles *in dubio mitius* and *in dubiis contra fiscum* adjudicated formerly by this court[149] and stating that in case there is no explicit legal regulations regarding the status of professional athletes (players) and their relationships with clubs, the court shall not use the legal interpretation obviously disadvantageous and unwanted by both contracting parties (the athlete and the club).

132. Consequently, according to this decision of the Supreme Administrative Court of Czech Republic, the athletes may use the status of self-employed persons if they have a properly issued trade licence (and therefore are able to use the 60% expenses flat rate) or they are entitled to perform their activities without the trade licence as members of the so-called independent professions. In such case the 40% expenses flat rate applies within the taxation of their income. Even though both variants of status of professional athletes are possible from the legal point of view, it is obvious which variant will be preferred by the professional athletes (players) as the first one is obviously fiscally favourable.

145. *See* § 7 s. 1 letter b) in connection with the § 7 s. 7 of the Act No. 586/1992 Coll., on income taxes, as amended.
146. *See* § 7 s. 2 letter c) in connection with § 7 s. 7 of the Act No. 586/1992 Coll., on income taxes, as amended.
147. *See* the Act No. 455/1991 Col., on trade entrepreneurship (Trade Licensing Act), as amended.
148. *See* the decision of the Supreme Administrative Court of Czech Republic, no. 6 Afs 278/2016 – 54, dated 13 Jul. 2017.
149. *See* the decision of the Supreme Administrative Court of Czech Republic, no. 2 Afs 16/2011 – 78, dated 29 Nov. 2011.

Part III. Doping and Sport

§1. The Czech Anti-doping Committee

133. The Czech Anti-doping Committee (ADV CR) is the expert Committee in charge of the fight against doping in sport on the territory of the Czech Republic. It was established by the Ministry of Education, Youth and Sport in 1999. The Czech Anti-doping Committee (ADV CR) is a contributory organization, i.e. non-profit organization fulfilling a particular public interest, of the Ministry of Education, Youth and Sport. The founding document has been issued by the ministry in 1999 and reissued again in the current wording in 2013.[150] According to this founding document ADV CR is the exclusive expert department with the scope of authority for the whole territory of the Czech Republic ensuring the execution of the anti-doping programme, including the whole concept of the anti-doping policy, its implementation, control mechanisms and education in the area of fight against doping in sport. To fulfil its purpose and to fulfil the goals of the International Anti-doping Policy in conformity with the World Anti-doping Code and International Convention against Doping in Sport, ADV CR mostly performs the following activities:

- preparing educational programmes and policies to promote sport competition without banned doping substances;
- organizing educational events;
- issuing guidelines and directives and lists of banned substances and methods;
- planning and executing the doping controls both during sporting competitions and at other times and providing analysis of the obtained samples;
- cooperating with sport organizations and national sport associations while imposing various anti-doping measures;
- participating on preparation of the national legislation and other documents connected with the fight against doping in sport;
- informing the Ministry of Education, Youth and Sports about the results of positive doping tests of athletes representing the Czech Republic internationally;
- participating on the activities of the international anti-doping institutions.

134. The statutory body of the ADV CR is the Director of ADV CR who is appointed and removed from the office by the Minister of Education, Youth and Sports.

150. The full wording of the founding document of the Czech Anti-doping Committee reissued by the Ministry of Education, Youth and Sports on 29 Mar. 2013 is available on the official website of the Czech Anti-doping Committee: (www.antidoping.cz), http://www.antidoping.cz/documents/zrizovaci_listina.pdf.

The Director of ADV CR manages, organizes and bears responsibility for the activities of the ADV CR while also directing its personnel politics. The Director of ADV CR is subordinate to the expert deputy in charge of the Section for Youth and Sport at the ministry and has a strong day-to-day connection to the Ministry of Education, Youth and Sports as he is methodically managed by the Director of the ministry's Department of Sport. The Director of ADV CR is responsible for the preparation and implementation of the anti-doping programme according to the International Convention against Doping in Sport in the Czech Republic and determines the strategy of communication regarding the anti-doping issues towards the general public. In conformity with the World Anti-doping Code the Director of ADV CR is responsible for: (i) the preparation of legislative measures regarding the doping control and the restraint of availability of doping substances to general public, (ii) the preparation of the conceptual materials and tools meant to enhance the education regarding the anti-doping matters at universities (sport and medicine specializations), (iii) the preparation of the long-term plan of the research tasks within the anti-doping matters. The Director of ADV CR enhances the long-term development of the anti-doping research and programme in the Czech Republic through the international cooperation (the development of new testing methods and laboratory procedures, the development of control of the banned substances, educational methods).

135. The Director of ADV CR also issues the organizational regulations which determine the organizational structure of ADV CR and establish the competence of its individual departments, while also being responsible for the personnel politics of ADV CR (for example granting the licences to the doping inspectors). The organizational regulations of ADV CR have to be approved by the expert deputy in charge of the Section for Youth and Sport at the Ministry of Education, Youth and Sports. The ADV CR as the contributory organization of the Ministry of Education, Youth and Sports does not own any real estate property and has been established for an indefinite period of time. The Director of ADV CR establishes the Committee for Therapeutic Exceptions and the Expert Council, while being automatically appointed the Chairman of the Expert Council.

136. The activities of ADV CR are based on the long-term anti-doping programme which helps to specify short-term tasks and goals set by the concrete one-year plans. These one-year plans are prepared in cooperation with the Czech national sports associations and following the recommendations of the international anti-doping organizations (namely WADA, UNESCO and the Council of Europe). The ADV CR is composed of several departments defined by the organizational regulations[151] issued by the Director of ADV CR.

The Department of doping controls and monitoring of ADV CR with the following main tasks:

- the planning and executing of the doping controls and cooperating with doping laboratories and national associations;
- carrying out the selection of the doping inspectors, providing of their continuous education and preparation, inspection and control of their work;

151. *See* the Organizational Regulations of the Czech Anti-doping Committee dated 3 Oct. 2013 on the official website of the Czech Anti-doping Committee (www.anti-doping.cz), http://www.antidoping.cz/documents/organizacni_rad.pdf.

- issuing of regulations, methodical information, lists of banned substances and medications according to the effective international regulations;
- cooperating with the Medical Committee of the International Olympic Committee (IOC), with WADA and with international sports associations;
- providing the agenda of the Committee for Therapeutic Exceptions.

The Department of education of ADV CR with the following main tasks:

- preparation of various educational programmes for the sports population;
- issuing of educational and promotional materials, organization of promotional events and lectures in cooperation with selected universities;
- cooperation with international organizations in the area of education, especially connected with IOC and the Council of Europe.

The Administrative department of ADV CR with the following main tasks:

- ensuring that the operational needs of ADV CR are met;
- being in charge of the economic agenda and the property of ADV CR;
- being in charge of the employees of ADV CR.

137. The Committee for Therapeutic Exceptions is the independent committee established by the Director of ADV CR based on the World Anti-doping Code and its international standard for therapeutic exceptions.[152] The Committee for Therapeutic Exceptions evaluates the requests of athletes with documented medical conditions to use medication containing the banned substance(s) or requests of athletes to use the banned methods according to the World Anti-doping Code and ascertains the legitimacy of the therapeutic exceptions in particular cases.

The decision of the Committee regarding the granting of the therapeutic exception, allowing the athlete to use medication containing a banned substance or to use a banned method, is binding and may be reviewed and changed only by WADA. The decision of the Committee regarding the rejection of the therapeutic exception may be appealed by the athlete to the Czech Olympic Committee or to the Court of Arbitration for Sport in Lausanne. The Chairman of the Committee for Therapeutic Exceptions is appointed or removed from office by the Director of ADV CR and the chairman may not be the employee of the ADV CR. The Committee for Therapeutic Exceptions has at least five or more members appointed for the time period of four years by the chairman of the Committee. The Chairman of the Committee summons and chairs the meetings of the Committee, while also being responsible for the decisions of the Committee. The Chairman of the Committee also represents the Committee externally. The members of the Committee are obliged to carry out their functions objectively and maintain confidentiality regarding all the matters connected with the Committee's work. The members of the Committee are obliged to comply with the stipulations of the World Anti-doping Code and with general legal regulations. In case there is any conflict of

152. The Committee for Therapeutic Exceptions does not have its own Statute. The basic rules governing the work of the Committee are contained in the Organizational Regulations of the Czech Anti-doping Committee.

interest in case of any member of the Committee, i.e. anything that prevents the member of the Committee from deciding the Committee matters objectively and independently, that member of the Committee is obliged to inform the Chairman of the Committee about this conflict of interest without any delay.

The agenda of the Committee is provided by the Department of doping controls and monitoring of ADV CR. The Committee is allowed to make decision with at least the Chairman and two members of the Committee present, while at least one of the present Committee members including the chairman has to be the expert in the area of the therapeutic exception which is under consideration. The decision which grants the therapeutic exception must be made unanimously, with the approval of all assessing members of the Committee including the chairman. The meetings of the Committee are not accessible to the general public, only the concerned athlete and his or her accompaniment may be present. The Committee is entitled to request external expert opinion or medical examination of the athlete with regard to the assessed matters. The decision which grants or rejects the therapeutic exception is sent to the athlete via registered post and the copy is always sent to WADA. The expenses and costs of the Committee's activities are born by the ADV CR.

§2. The Directive on Control and Sanctioning of Doping in Sport

138. The Directive on control and sanctioning of doping in sport issued by the ADV CR is the main regulation concerning the anti-doping movement in the Czech Republic and has been issued following the ratification of the International Convention against Doping in Sport by the Czech Republic. The International Convention against Doping in Sport determines the responsibilities and obligations of the national anti-doping organizations (ADV CR in the Czech Republic) regarding the fight against doping in their respective countries. The World Anti-doping Code as a part of the International Convention against doping in Sport has been ratified by the Czech Republic and subsequently published in the Collection of International Treaties[153] (No. 46/2008). According to the World Anti-doping Code (Article 20.5.2) the national anti-doping organization is obliged to implement and execute anti-doping policy and rules compatible with the World Anti-doping Code, therefore ADV CR independently plans, coordinates and performs doping controls, advocates its necessity and usefulness, cooperates with the national sports associations, reciprocally cooperates with other national anti-doping organizations on doping controls abroad and investigates the violations of anti-doping regulations and potential involvement of people in doping cases. The introduction to the Directive expressly states that the anti-doping rules are the same as rules of competitions in which the athletes participate, therefore by participating only, the athletes accept that they are bound by these anti-doping rules and no other legal act is necessary for these rules to become binding for the athletes. The introduction to the Directive also states that the anti-doping rules are not restricted by usual legal standards of criminal procedural law or employment law.

153. The international treaties ratified by the Czech Republic are published in the Collection of International Treaties. The laws are published in the Collection of Laws.

The Directive itself contains the following word for word stipulations obligatorily adopted from the World Anti-doping Code: (1.) The definition of doping, (2.) Anti-doping rule violations, (3.) Proof of doping, (4.2.2) Specific substances, (4.3.3) Decision of WADA on including the substances on Prohibited List, (7.11) Retirement from sport, (9.) The automatic disqualification of individual results, (10.) Sanctions on individuals, (11.) Consequences to teams, (13.) Appeals – except for articles 13.2.2, 13.6 and 13.7, (15.1) Application and recognition of decisions, (17.) Statue of limitations, (24.) Interpretation of the Code and Appendix 1. – Definitions.

139. The proceedings in the doping cases are regulated by the Article 8 of the Directive (8.) – disciplinary proceedings. The Directive acknowledges a major role of national sports associations within the anti-doping proceedings as in case of the anti-doping rule violation it is the national sports association that opens the disciplinary proceedings with the athlete who has allegedly violated the anti-doping rule. The national sports association obligatorily opens disciplinary proceedings with any athlete who has been informed by the ADV CR about the alleged anti-doping rule violation. The explicitly acknowledged purpose of these disciplinary proceedings is to determine, whether the anti-doping rule has been violated by the athlete.

The Directive itself states that the disciplinary proceedings held by the national sports association need to respect the right of the athlete for fair proceedings while honouring the following key principles:

- the right for timely proceedings;
- fair and impartial decision-making tribunal;
- the right to be represented by a legal representative at one's own costs;
- the right to be informed in the proper way and timely about the allegation regarding the breach of anti-doping rules;
- the right to make statement with regard to the allegation regarding the breach of anti-doping rules and its consequences;
- the right to suggest evidence and to question the witnesses;
- the right to have an interpreter present during the proceedings, while the decision-making tribunal determines who bears the costs of this interpreter;
- the right to receive timely written decision including the reasoning behind any imposed ineligibility.

These above-mentioned key principles contained in the Directive need to be complied with, however each particular disciplinary proceeding opened by the national sports association are held according to the disciplinary rules of this particular national sports association. Typically, the body holding these proceedings is the Disciplinary Committee of the relevant national sports association. This Disciplinary Committee however usually deals with a very specific violations of sports rules within one particular area of sport[154] and the interpretation and application of very specific, complex and sometimes complicated legal rules contained within the Directive may be beyond the scope of its expertise. This has caused some problems in the past as the members of the disciplinary committees often without a legal education dealing usually with violations of specific technical rules repeatedly on week-to-week basis found the Directive too difficult to interpret and to apply on a particular case, rendering the first instance decision void or without a proper reasoning. This led to the case being effectively decided by the appeal tribunal, in the doping cases the Arbitration Committee of the Czech Olympic Committee. Even though the further appeal in some cases is possible (to CAS), this meant that the very important question of the violation of the anti-doping rule with ultimate consequences regarding the athlete's further career was effectively decided by a competent body only in the second instance (during the appeal procedure).

§3. The Private Regulation of the National Sports Associations

140. The national private regulation of anti-doping is centred in the Directive and the activities of the Anti-doping Committee of the Czech Republic. The national sports associations generally used to have mostly very brief rules regarding the breach of anti-doping rules by players or eventually by others, usually incorporated in their Disciplinary Regulations, but the trend seems to lead to exchanging these brief rules originating at the national sports association by references to the Directive. For example, the Disciplinary Regulations of the Football Association of Czech Republic effective as of 1 July 2017 contain two disciplinary violations connected with banned substances. The first one is aimed at players who in case of using a substance banned by the Czech Anti-doping Committee (this substance is on the list of banned substances issued by the Czech Anti-doping Committee), may be sanctioned by ineligibility for the time period from one month up to ten years, by a ban on participating on any activities of the Football Association of Czech Republic for the time period from one year up to ten years, by expulsion from the Football Association of Czech Republic or by a fine in the amount up to CZK 5,000,000.[155] The second disciplinary violation aims at anyone who produces, sells, stores, or otherwise supplies to himself or to a third person a banned substance. This person may be punished by ineligibility for a time period from two months up to twenty years, by a ban on participating on any activities of the Football Association of Czech Republic for a time period from one year up to twenty

154. Typically, the Disciplinary Committee of the Czech Football Associations deals with the violations of the rules of the game, misconduct of fans at football stadiums, etc. while the Disciplinary Committee of the Autoclub of Czech Republic deals with the violations of regulations regarding the rules of automobile and motorcycle racing. Every branch of sport has its own differently complex technical regulations, however while dealing with these on weekly basis, the disciplinary committees of the national sports associations may be rightly considered experts in applying these regulations. On the contrary, the disciplinary committees usually do not apply the anti-doping regulations, because the doping cases are infrequent. Given this the disciplinary committees have difficulties with the application of the anti-doping rules, often feeling too protective of 'their' athlete and perceiving the internationally approved two- or four-year sanctions as too harsh.

155. Approximately EUR 200,000.

years, by expulsion from the Football Association of Czech Republic, or by a fine in the amount up to CZK 10 million.[156]

However, in the Disciplinary Regulations of the Football Association of Czech Republic effective as of 6 December 2017 these two disciplinary violations have been replaced by a simple sentence stating: 'Anyone who will violate the anti-doping rules according to the Directive, will be sanctioned according to the Directive.'[157]

141. Very similarly, the current Competition and Disciplinary Regulations issued by the Czech Ice Hockey Association acknowledge the breach of the anti-doping rule by an individual (in general described as playing under the influence of a banned substance, breach of the ban on doping, inducing others to use a banned substance, etc.) and by a team (in general described as playing under the influence of a banned substance or a breach of the ban on doping). In both cases the Competition and Disciplinary Regulations do not determine the sanction, but state that the sanction will be imposed in both simple and more serious cases according to a specific regulation, which is the Directive on control and sanctioning of doping in sport issued by the ADV CR.[158]

§4. THE ROMAN KREUZIGER CASE

142. The above-mentioned uncertainty of the national sport association with regard to the applicable rules and the obvious complexity of the case itself proved to be a factor in the case of Roman Kreuziger, a Czech professional cyclist, who has been accused of the violation of anti-doping rule by the International Cycling Union (UCI) in June 2013. The suggested violation of anti-doping rule was based on irregularities in the athlete's haematological profile contained in his biological passport during 2011 and 2012. These irregularities led UCI to the conclusion that it is highly likely that the athlete has used a prohibited substance. The UCI subsequently initiated disciplinary proceedings against the athlete and provisionally suspended the athlete from all competitions. According to the Anti-doping Rules of the International Cycling Union (UCI ADR) valid at the time, the disciplinary proceedings against the athlete were supposed to be held by the national federation of the licence holder (athlete),[159] in this case the Czech Cycling Union. The Czech Cycling Union, however, in conformity with the Article 257 of UCI ADR, which allowed the national federation to refer a case to an external hearing panel, decided to refer the case to the Arbitration Committee of the Czech Olympic Committee. The president of the Czech Cycling Union was cited in the media saying that the case was too complicated and should be decided by

156. *See* the para. 52 ss 1 and 2 of the Disciplinary Code of the Football Association of Czech Republic effective as of 1 Jul. 2017.

157. *See* the new para. 52 of the Disciplinary Code of the Football Association of Czech Republic effective as of 16 Dec. 2017 at the official website of FACR (www.fotbal.cz), https://facr.fotbal.cz/uredni-deska-predpisy/195?category=1.

158. *See* the Amendment 2 (the Disciplinary offences and sanctions) to the Competition and Disciplinary Regulations of the Czech Ice Hockey Association valid and effective as of 18 Jun. 2016 at http://www.cslh.cz/text/121-stanovy-a-rady.html.

159. *See* Art. 234 of the Anti-doping Rules of the International Cycling Union valid in 2014.

experts in anti-doping cases as he has personally read the file and did not understand it.[160] Technically the jurisdiction of the Arbitration Committee of COV was established by the Arbitration Agreement stipulated between the athlete, the Czech Cycling Union and the Czech Olympic Committee and this was historically the first time when the Arbitration Committee of COV decided a case as the first instance hearing panel or tribunal, however under very specific legal conditions.

As stated above, the UCI ADR permitted the case to be referred by the national federation to an external hearing panel while stating that in such case the external hearing panel agrees to resolve the case under the UCI ADR while using its own procedural rules. These procedural rules however, are also to a certain extent modified by UCI ADR. Most importantly, because of these very specific modifications the proceedings at the Arbitration Committee of COV, generally not bound by any time limits, had to be finished within one month of the dispatch of the notice of initiation of the proceedings to the parties.

143. Typically, in the proceedings held by the Arbitration Committee of COV: (i) the athlete suspect of violation of the anti-doping rule, (ii) the national sport association whose body (usually the disciplinary committee) decided the case in the first instance and (iii) the Anti-doping Committee of Czech Republic (ADV CR) are the parties.[161] In this case within the disciplinary proceedings held by the Arbitration Committee of COV according to the UCI ADR: (i) the athlete and (ii) the Czech Cycling Union were parties to the proceedings with full procedural rights. With the consent of the parties, the representative of the ADV CR was invited to participate in the proceedings as an observer without procedural rights and at the end of the oral hearing presented his statement regarding the case. As a result, the ADV CR was extraordinarily not a regular party to the proceedings in this anti-doping case. The UCI, while also not being a regular party to the proceedings before the Arbitration Committee, had substantial procedural rights grounded in the UCI ADR.[162] It is obvious that these strong procedural rights of UCI were more typical for the disciplinary proceedings before the membership national federation of UCI, where UCI has a more supervisory position, than for the standard proceedings held before the Arbitration Committee of COV.

144. The UCI, even though not a regular party to the proceedings, sent several written statements regarding the case and participated within the proceedings held by the Arbitration Committee to an extent in a very active way, while also maintaining a certain distance by deciding not to send a representative to the oral hearing taking place during the proceedings. The Czech Cycling Union, while a regular party to the proceedings, sent its representative to the oral hearing, but remained very passive, not

160. *See* https://sport.idnes.cz/verdikt-kreuziger-039-/cyklistika.aspx?c=A140922_134459_cyklistika_tm2.

161. *See* the Procedural Rules of the Arbitration Committee of COV available at the official website of the Czech Olympic Committee: (www.olympic.cz), https://www.olympic.cz/upload/files/Jednaci-rad-RK-COV.pdf.

162. For example the right to receive the copy of the documentation of the case, the right to give an opinion and demand that a sanction be imposed, either in writing or at the hearing, the right to request that the oral hearing in the proceedings is not held before the UCI has received the complete case file and additional strong procedural rights.

presenting statements and leaving the actual proposals as to the sanctioning of the athlete in the hands of the UCI. As the Czech Cycling Union repeatedly referred to the statements and proposals of the UCI, the Arbitration Committee technically considered these statements and proposals as made by the Czech Cycling Union, the regular party to the proceedings with full procedural rights.

145. The proceedings were highly influenced by the lack of time given that the Arbitration Committee had to abide by the one-month time limit provided by the UCI ADR for the disciplinary proceedings held before the body of the national federation. Because of this, the athlete repeatedly pleaded, both during the oral hearing and in written statements, a breach of his right to a fair trial, stating that he had insufficient time to properly prepare and to respond to statements of the UCI. The athlete also requested that the statements and evidence sent by the UCI would not be taken into consideration by the Arbitration Committee. Surprisingly enough, the UCI claimed the very same things, saying it had not enough time to respond to the athlete's statements provided in the Czech language and complaining that the deadlines during the proceedings were too short, therefore effectively questioning the principles adopted by the Arbitration Committee into the proceedings from UCI ADR. The UCI also requested that the statements and evidence provided by the athlete in his final motion were not taken into consideration by the Arbitration Committee. On the contrary, the UCI's legal counsel repeatedly advised the Arbitration Committee that it should strictly follow the UCI ADR and even resorted to voicing concerns as to the impartiality and independence of the members of the Arbitration Committee. The UCI was obviously abusing its strong and specific position within these proceedings ensured by the unbalanced stipulations of the UCI ADR.

146. While pointing out that the short duration of the proceedings was caused by the rules provided by the UCI, the Arbitration Committee stated that all the statements and evidence provided by the parties and UCI will be taken into consideration to ensure that the case itself is assessed and decided in the most just and fair manner possible. It was also further stated by the Arbitration Committee that the UCI ADR are not suitable to provide a fair trial with an athlete accused of the violation of the anti-doping rule, as the rules suffer from excessively short deadlines for rendering the decision, entirely absent basic procedures and probably the worst defect – the unilateral preference for UCI's procedural position (although UCI is not even the party to the proceedings). It was therefore very difficult for the Arbitration Committee to follow the UCI ADR and simultaneously provide all the parties to the proceedings with a fair trial.

147. It is interesting, that in this case even though the abnormalities or irregularities in the athlete's biological passport were considered the main evidence of his supposed violation of the anti-doping rules, the values of the relevant indicators (in this case the values of haemoglobin and reticulocytes) have never exceeded the baseline values in the athlete's biological passport. The athlete argued that the abnormalities in his biological passport can be fully explained by his medical condition (hypothyroidism – a disorder of the endocrine system in which the thyroid gland does not produce enough thyroid hormone[163]) and its treatment (using gradually increasing doses of L-thyroxin), which could have caused a change in the values in the athlete's biological

163. Hypothyroidism can cause a number of symptoms – poor ability to tolerate cold, a feeling of tiredness, constipation, depression, weight gain, etc.

passport. The UCI on the contrary argued that given the irregularities in the athlete's biological passport the probability of the violation of the anti-doping rule by the athlete was highly likely. Given the short time of the proceedings both parties presented extensive expert evidence supporting their respective statements. The expert evidence basically focused on the question, whether the treatments the athlete received for his hypothyroidism could have caused the abnormalities in the athlete's biological passport. This was confirmed by the expert opinions provided by the athlete and completely rejected by the presented expert opinions of the expert panel on the side of UCI, leading to obvious contradiction within the conclusions of the expert opinions. Facing the one-month deadline to complete the proceedings according to the UCI ADR the Arbitration Committee decided that there was no time to ask an impartial expert to provide the evaluation of the conclusions of the existing expert opinions and decided to focus on the assessment of the existing evidence.

148. According to the Article 22 of the UCI ADR, the UCI and the national federation (Czech Cycling Union) bear the burden of proof to establish that the violation of an anti-doping rule has occurred on the side of the athlete. The normal standard of proof in the doping cases is the comfortable satisfaction of the tribunal, being a greater standard of proof than a mere balance of probability used in civil matters, but also lower standard than proof beyond the reasonable doubt typical for criminal cases.

This turned out to be the crucial matter within the proceedings as the Arbitration Committee reached the conclusion that neither the Czech Cycling Union nor the UCI had borne the burden of proof as to the assertion that the athlete had violated an anti-doping rule and had decided that Roman Kreuziger has not committed any violation of the UCI ADR.[164] This decision, though at the time may have seemed controversial and UCI and WADA both appealed the decision to CAS in accordance with the Article 330 of UCI ADR, however remained the final one, as both UCI and WADA later withdrew their appeals and the athlete resumed his professional career in cycling.[165] The reasons given publicly for the withdrawal of the appeal by both organizations were 'the availability of newly obtained information, which led to conclusion that, in accordance with the applicable UCI anti-doping rules and WADA Athlete Biological Passport [ABP] operating guidelines, there is at this stage no basis to proceed further'.[166]

149. This was not the first time the national federation's arbitral panel has decided that the evidence based on the athlete's biological passport is not sufficient proof to state the anti-doping rule violation, however these decisions have been later overruled by CAS,[167] which repeatedly accepted evidence in the athlete's biological

164. The complete version of the arbitration award in case of Roman Kreuziger, file no. 03/2014, issued by the Arbitration Committee of the Czech Olympic Committee on 22 Sep. 2014, including the grounds for the decision, is available on the website of the Czech Olympic Committee (www.olympic.cz), http://www.olympic.cz/upload/files/x5lpqjac5a-KREUZIGER-ROZH-N.pdf.

165. *See* http://www.skysports.com/cycling/news/21683/9876397/roman-kreuziger-cleared-of-doping-after-uci-and-wada-drop-case.

166. *See* http://www.sportsintegrityinitiative.com/uci-wada-end-appeal-against-decision-to-acquit-kreuziger/.

167. *See* CAS 2010/A/2235, UCI v. Tadej Valjaveo & Olympic Committee of Slovenia and CAS 2010/A/2308 and 2011/A/2335, Pellizotti v. CONI & UCI, UCI v. Pellizoto, FCI, CONI.

passport as proving the anti-doping violation. However, in case of Roman Kreuziger's biological passport, where the indicators, while showing irregularities, have never exceeded the baseline values and where the athlete has provided expert opinions supporting his theory that these irregularities were caused by his medical conditions and its treatment, the decision of CAS could in this sense have been ground breaking. Implying that this could have been a factor in the decision of the UCI and WADA to withdraw their appeals to maintain the unbeaten position of the athlete's biological passport within the CAS jurisprudence is merely a speculation. The aggressive conduct of UCI during the proceedings supported by the unbalanced stipulations of the applicable regulations issued by UCI (UCI ADR), however brings many questions regarding the balance between the fight against doping in cycling (and sport in general) and the fundamental rights of cyclists (and athletes in general) for the fair trial. The case of Roman Kreuziger was the last case of anti-doping violation in international cycling decided by the body of the national federation as the UCI decided to change its own regulations and create the Anti-doping Tribunal with the following reasoning published at the UCI's website: 'The UCI Anti-doping Tribunal takes over the task, previously delegated by the UCI to the National Federations, of handling disciplinary proceedings and rendering decisions concerning violations of the Anti-doping Regulations. In principle, the jurisdiction of the UCI Anti-doping Tribunal is limited to anti-doping affairs involving international level riders. The judges are fully independent from the UCI and were nominated in view of their outstanding expertise in the field of anti-doping and dispute resolution.'[168]

168. *See* the official website of UCI: http://www.uci.ch/news/article/anti-doping-tribunal/.

Part IV. Sport and Commerce

Chapter 1. General Issues

150. Within the territory of the European Union sport is considered to be an important public activity with many benefits. According to the EU White Paper on Sport, it was estimated that in 2004 the sport had added value of EUR 407 billion in the EU, representing 3.7% of the European Union's GDP. In addition, sport created places for 5.4% of the workforce. Within the Czech Republic's economy, the sector of sport (excluding offsetting effects) in terms of GDP and employment is comparable to for example the production of motor vehicles, trailers and semi-trailers, agriculture, forestry and fishing, manufacture of food products, production of rubber and plastic products, mining or production of chemicals and preparations. The share of sport in the Czech Republic's state budget is estimated at 3.3%, the share of sport (including multiplier effects) in the GDP of the Czech Republic is about 2.7%. The total average annual contribution to the public sector was about CZK 52 billion in 2011.[169]

151. In addition to the economic effect, the benefits of sport in general are much broader, especially in a small country as the Czech Republic. Among these we may consider especially the marketing benefits:

- The extraordinary sports performances at an international events of great importance (e.g. the gold medal of Czech hockey players from the 1998 Nagano Winter Olympics Games is legendary and became the part of Czech Republic's national folklore, the victory of the tennis player Petra Kvitová in Wimbledon final 2011, etc.) – these events tend to unite the Czech public in a way nothing else can.
- The participation of representatives in international sports competitions – participation of Czech athletes in matches abroad increases the international awareness of the Czech Republic.
- The exceptional sports personalities – the Czech athletes who achieve excellent performances on the international scene on a regular and long-term basis (e.g. ice hockey player Jaromír Jágr, football players Pavel Nedvěd and Petr Čech, tennis player Petra Kvitová).

169. *See* Koncepce financování sportu v České republice – Analyticko-koncepční studie ('The Policy of Financing Sport in Czech Republic – Analytical Conceptual Study') by KPMG Česká republika, s.r.o., dated 13 Mar. 2012, available at http://www.olympic.cz/financovani/docs/koncepce_financovani_sportu_prezentace_v9a.pdf.

- The sports events of international importance – sports events organized in the Czech Republic, TV rights abroad (e.g. Prague International Marathon, Grand Prix of the Czech Republic, etc.).

152. Among the other general benefits of sport in the Czech Republic we may consider the health benefits (the prevention of civilization diseases, the healthier lifestyle of general public), the benefits in the field of education (the physical education in schools, the physical activities in local community clubs, the education through sport has positive effects among socially disadvantaged groups, etc.) and the social benefits:

- the social integration regardless of age, gender, nationality; sport significantly affects the position of young people, people with disabilities or people from disadvantaged backgrounds;
- due to the great interest not only among young people, sport creates a strong potential for promoting collective association and cooperation in various economic and social areas;
- sport leads to the development of respect for others in the team, observance of the rules of the game, solidarity, discipline, observance of fair play principles.

Chapter 2. Public Regulation

§1. Media and TV Rights

153. Currently, the payments from TV rights are without any doubt the most important source of income for sports in general. Within Europe for example the revenues from the English Premier League TV rights steadily increase since 1992 and between 2013 and 2016 the Premier League generated over 3 billion pounds in revenue from the marketing of its broadcasting rights. However, for the 2016–2019 period a further increase was inevitable and the TV rights for Premier League were sold for the amount exceeding 5 billion pounds.[170] Football is now the most broadcasted sport in Europe and is very popular among viewers. The same applies for the Czech Republic, where football is generally the most TV broadcasted sports venue with the exception of top sports events where the Czech athletes traditionally participate (the World Cup Ice Hockey Final, the biathlon races, etc.).

154. In Czech Republic the television market consists of the following types of television channels:

- the public television (ČT (Czech TV) TV[171] channels) – the public service television is funded by fees paid by household and entrepreneurs owning televisions and radio receivers;[172]
- the commercial TV (Nova,[173] Prima,[174] etc.) – these are private TV stations that are funded mainly by advertising revenues;
- the pay TV (UPC,[175] O2 TV,[176] Digi[177]).

At the same time, the most watched sports in the Czech Republic are football, ice hockey and biathlon. While ice hockey and biathlon are fully available on the public television channels (mostly the special public sports channel – ČT Sport), the broadcasting rights to the top professional football league of Czech Republic[178] are divided between the public television (ČT Sport) and the paid O2 TV channel (with the right to choose the most attractive match of the respective league round) and web (internet) channel isport.cz.[179] Therefore, during the last couple of seasons the most attractive matches

170. *See* the article Premier League TV broadcasting rights revenue* from 1992 to 2019 (in million GBP) at https://www.statista.com/statistics/385002/premier-league-tv-rights-revenue/.
171. http://www.ceskatelevize.cz/.
172. *See* the Act. No. 348/2005 Coll., on television and broadcasting fees, as amended.
173. http://tv.nova.cz/.
174. http://www.iprima.cz/.
175. www.upc.cz.
176. www.o2tv.cz.
177. www.cz.digi.cz.
178. www.hetliga.cz.
179. https://isport.blesk.cz/.

in the first professional football league are available only on private channels or on the internet against a one-time payment, following the trend common in Europe.

155. The broadcasting rights to the first professional football league of Czech Republic were in the past transferred to STES, a.s., the marketing company of the Czech Football Association (FACR) and STES, a.s. negotiated the deals with the potential buyers. Following the establishing the League Football Association (LFA) the television rights should be (starting from the 2018/2019 season) marketed and sold by the LFA, while continuing the trend of the attractive matches to be sold to private channels with the goal of continually increasing the revenues from the television rights for the first professional football league in the Czech Republic. Currently, the television and media rights to the first professional football league in Czech Republic generate significantly lower revenues in comparison with the leagues in countries with comparable media markets. Though never made public, it is estimated that the television rights for the first professional football league in the Czech Republic cost approximately 4,2 million euro per season. The media rights of the Austrian and Hungarian leagues are evaluated approximately five times, the Polish and the Belgian leagues nine times and the Dutch competitions almost thirteen times better than the first professional football league in the Czech Republic.

§2. Sponsoring

156. Unlike the donation contract, the sponsorship agreement is not regulated as a special contractual type within the Czech law. The donation contract on the contrary, is a contract with terms regulated by the Civil Code,[180] as one of the typical contractual types. The essential characteristics of the donation contract are the voluntariness and the transfer of ownership free of charge. Within the Czech law, the sponsorship agreement is, on the contrary, considered to be the so-called *innominate contract*, or the unnamed contract.[181]

157. The legal definition of sponsorship in the Czech law may be found in the paragraph 1 Article 4 of the Act on the Regulation of Advertising,[182] which defines this term in the following way:

> 'The sponsorship means a contribution made in order to support the production or sale of goods, services, or other sponsorship performance. A sponsor is a legal or natural person who provides such a contribution for that purpose.'

Following this definition, sadly the only definition of sponsoring within the Czech legal system, we cannot substitute the sponsorship contract and the donation contract, but we may also not substitute the sponsorship with the advertising. In the Czech law the sponsorship is considered as something halfway in between the donation and the

---

180. *See* §§ 2055 et seq. of the Act No. 89/2012 Coll., the Civil Code, as amended.
181. *See* § 1756 of the Act No. 89/2012 Coll., the Civil Code, as amended, which enables the contracting parties to stipulate a contract, which is not regulated by the Civil Code as a contractual type.
182. *See* § 1 Art. 4 of the Act No. 40/1995 Coll., on the regulation of advertising, as amended.

advertising. The sponsorship contract is not free of charge – the sponsor provides its contribution in order to support its entrepreneurial activity, however not by simply advertising its products or services, but more by improving its public image by connecting itself or himself with the sports organization or the particular athlete, therefore consequently improving the visibility of the sponsor's products or services. With regard to the above-mentioned and from the point of view of the income taxation the earnings of the club and/or athlete based on the sponsorship (i.e. support of sport for the counter-service) must be considered as the advertisement revenue.

§3. Merchandising

158. The merchandising is a relatively young and modern business-marketing discipline. Merchandising can be defined as sales promotion, as a complex, consisting of sales measures made by the manufacturer by trading. Different definitions, comparing merchandising with marketing, describe merchandising as sales promotion.[183] In the Czech Republic, in the area of sport, the term merchandising is understood in particular as the presentation (sale) of products with the logo of a particular sports club or other gift items to its fans and general public. Most common souvenirs in football and ice hockey are replicas of the club jerseys, other clothing, shirts, the traditional football scarfs, ice hockey caps, etc. However, even though all professional clubs in football and ice hockey sell their merchandising, the merchandising revenues of the clubs in the Czech Republic in comparison with foreign clubs (mainly in comparison with clubs in the top leagues in Europe) are insignificant. These revenues of the Czech football and ice hockey clubs from merchandising are estimated at about 3%–4% of the club's yearly income, and therefore negligible in terms of creating the club's seasonal budget. Most of the merchandising products are sold in the fan shops situated at the stadiums or very close to them and over the internet in the clubs e-shops. Most Czech clubs are also known to outsource the merchandising to specialized companies in exchange for a percentage of the profit.

§4. The Ownership of Clubs

159. In the terms of the Czech law, we may define the following basic forms of legal entities – (i) the associations and (ii) the corporations (especially limited liability company and joint-stock company). The associations are the most common legal form of citizens' association in the Czech Republic. As the association we generally understand the association of persons, where the essential principles of such association are self-government, voluntary membership and separation of property of the association from the assets of its respective members. The purpose of the association are most often mutually beneficial objectives, i.e. joint activities aimed only towards the members of

183. *See* PhDr. Ladislav Bedřich, CSc., Fakulta sportovních studií Masarykovy univerzity, Katedra Kinantropologie (The Faculty of Sports Studies of the Masaryk University, Department of Kinanthropology) [online], 2007 Marketing ve sportu (Marketing in sport) https://is.muni.cz/elportal/estud/fsps/ps07/mark/pages/03.html#n02.

the association (sports clubs, hunting associations, etc.) or publicly beneficial objectives towards the general public (provision of social services, educational and information activities, etc.). Of course these two objectives are often mixed to a certain degree. The association may also engage in business on its own behalf, but it cannot be its principal activity, and any profits hereof must be used to support the association's own aims. The members of the association may be both natural and legal persons as well.

160. The business corporations governed by the Czech law are legal entities. The Business Corporations Act[184] divides the commercial companies into personal companies and capital companies. The fundamental difference between personal and capital companies is that while all or at least some of the partnerships are liable for the company's debts unlimitedly, by all property and in solidarity, the shareholders of the capital companies are either not liable for the company's debts at all or their liability is limited. Private companies are the public company and the limited partnership, the capital companies are the limited liability company and the joint-stock company. In addition to these, there is also the European company and the European economic interest group, as well as the cooperatives and the European cooperative society. The cooperatives, which are among the capital business corporations, are different from the commercial companies mainly because the cooperatives are not typical business entities; however, the law allows the cooperatives to be set up for business purposes as well. Another significant difference from the commercial companies is that the cooperatives have the unmatched number of members (i.e. the possibility of accessing and exiting for members of a cooperative without the need to change the amount of the registered capital in accordance with the statutory procedure rules) and hence a very flexible amount of the share capital. Although cooperatives are required to form share capital, it is not recorded in the public Czech commercial register and its amount is variable in relation to the current number of members and the amount of their respective member deposits.

161. All kinds of corporations are generally accepted within the legal regulation of sport therefore it is up to the decision of the concerned subjects which legal form they will choose for their activity. However, on the professional level the national sport associations (usually within their licensing systems) usually demand a certain legal form of their members to allow them to participate in competitions they organize. This is typical for football, where these often very strict licensing regulations are based on the principles determined in the Regulations of UEFA and FIFA binding for their member associations. According to the licensing regulations of the Football Association of Czech Republic, all professional clubs participating in the first professional football league and the second professional football league in the Czech Republic are obliged to have the legal form of the joint-stock company.[185] This is determined in accordance with the Article 45 of the Club Licensing Code, which states:

184. *See* the Act no. 90/2012 Coll., on business corporation (the business corporations act), as amended.

185. *See* Klubový licenční řád FAČR, Edice 2017 ('FAČR Club Licensing Regulations, Edition 2017), at the official website of club licensing of the Football Association of Czech Republic: (www.clublicensing.cz), http://www.clublicensing.cz/wp-content/uploads/2014/08/161212-KLRad-Edice-2017.pdf.

> The license applicant may be only a football club, i.e. a legal entity which has the status of a 'joint stock company' according to the Commercial Code and its shares are issued only as the registered shares. The license applicant, who is a newcomer to the FAČR's second highest competition, is subject to this condition from the beginning of 2 years after entering the second highest competition of FAČR.

The mandatory legal form of a joint-stock company for clubs that participate in the two highest professional football competitions of the Czech Republic has been established in 1996. Before that, some clubs used the legal form of the limited liability company. Following 1996 the clubs were still able to issue bearer shares, which did not help with the increase of transparency of the ownership of football clubs. However, following the Act on Transparency[186] which has become effective on 1 January 2014, the clubs are obliged to issue only registered shares. Therefore, the clubs are obliged to keep the list of shareholders and the concealment of the ownership structure has become much more difficult. Additionally, the club that has the legal form of a joint stock company must, of course, comply with all legal requirements imposed on this legal form pursuant to the Business Corporation Act, including accounting regulations (e.g. audit requirement), etc.

162. In comparison, the clubs playing in the top basketball league in the Czech Republic (National Basketball League) and in the top professional ice hockey league in the Czech Republic (Ice Hockey Extraliga) are not obliged to have a specific mandatory legal form. The top ice hockey clubs mostly use the status of the limited liability company and the joint-stock company. In basketball there is even more differentiation as apart from the limited liability companies and the joint-stock companies some clubs in the top basketball league use the legal status of associations.

163. The statutes of FACR also involve a strict rule regarding the ownership of a football club by one person,[187] stating:

> One of the special obligations of a football club is the obligation to ensure:
>
> ....
>
> b) the fulfilment of the requirement to ensure that one person may in only one membership club directly or indirectly:

---

186. The Act No. 134/2013 Coll., on some measures to increase the transparency of the joint-stock companies (Act on Transparency), as amended, effectively discontinued previously in Czech Republic very popular use of the bearer shares, which enabled joint-stock companies to conceal their ownership structure and were also very easily transferred to another owner.

187. *See* Art. 16 s. 6 letter b) of the current valid and effective Statutes of the Football Association of Czech Republic approved by the General Assembly of FACR on 2 Jun. 2017 on the official website of FACR: www.fotbal.cz.

aa) have 50 % and more voting rights, the determination of the voting rights does not take into account any restriction of the voting rights resulting from the agreements, decisions of the bodies of the member club or founder's legal conduct;

bb) own a share of 50 % or higher.

...

Thus to some extent mirroring the relevant stipulation of the UEFA Regulations regarding the participation of clubs in the UEFA Europa League[188] and the UEFA Champions League.[189]

164. In comparison, the relevant rules[190] of the Czech Basketball Federation approach the topic of possible dual ownership of clubs more vaguely, stating:

> Two teams of the same club cannot participate in the NBL,[191] more precisely two clubs whose owner, co-owner or a statutory representative is the same natural or legal person.

165. The Czech Ice Hockey Federation (CSLH) has no rules limiting the dual ownership of the clubs at all.

188. *See* Art. 5 (Integrity of Competition) of Regulations of the UEFA Europa League 2015-2018 cycle, 2017/2018 season, available at the official site of UEFA: http://www.uefa.com/uefaeuropaleague/news/newsid=2467157.html#/.

189. *See* Art. 5 (Integrity of Competition) of Regulations of the UEFA Champions League 2015-2018 cycle, 2017/2018 season, available at the official site of UEFA: https://www.uefa.com/insideuefa/documentlibrary/regulations/index.html.

190. *See* Part A, Art. 7 of the document Sportovně technické podmínky účasti v soutěžích (Sports technical conditions for participation in competitions) issued by the Czech Basketball Federation (CBF), available on the official website of the NBF: (www.cbf.cz), http://www.cbf.cz/files/140715MTd.pdf.

191. The National Basketball League (NBL) is the top basketball league in Czech Republic.

Selected Bibliography

Bach, David: *1001 Financial Words You Need to Know*, Oxford University Press, USA, 2003.

Bělina, M., Drápal, L. a kol.: *Zákoník práce. Komentář. (The Labor Code. Commentary.)*, 2. Edition, C. H. Beck, Praha, 2015.

Colucci, Michele (ed.): *The FIFA Regulations on Working with Intermediaries. Its implementation on national level.*, Sports Law and Policy Centre, 2015.

Hamerník, Pavel: *Sportovní právo s mezinárodním prvkem (Sports law with the international element)*, Auditorium, Praha, 2007.

Hamerník, Pavel: *Sportovní právo – Hledání rovnováhy mezi specifickou sportovní úpravou a platným právem (Sports law: Finding the balance between the specific sports regulation and law and positive law)*, Ústav státu a práva AV ČR, Praha, 2012.

Jakubcová, Kristina: *Sport a olympijské hnutí v zemích Visegrádu, jejich vývoj a transformace v postkomunistické éře (Sport and olympic movement in the Visegrad countries, it's evolution and tranformation in the post-communist era)*, Univerzita Karlova v Praze, Nakladatelství Carolinum, Praha, 2012.

Jánošíková, Petra; Mrkývka, Petr; Tomažič, Ivan: *Finanční a daňové právo. (Financial and Tax Law)*, Aleš Čeněk, Plzeň, 2009.

Kössl, Jiří, Krátký, František, Marek, Jaroslav: *Dějiny tělesné výchovy II. (History of physical education II.)*, Olympia, Praha, 1986.

Kössl, Jiří: *Historie Českého olympijského výboru a olympijského hnutí, Obnovení Českého Olympijského výboru dne 21. 12. 1992 (The History of the Czech Olympic Movement, The Restoration of the Czech Olympic Committee on 21st December, 1992)*, ČOV, Praha, 1993.

Králík, Michal: *Civilní a trestní odpovědnost sportovců za sportovní úrazy (The civil and criminal liability of athletes in case of sports injuries)*, Nakladatelství Leges, Praha, 2016.

Králík, Michal: *Civilní odpovědnost sportovců za sportovní úrazy (The civil liability of athletes in case of sports injuries)*, Nakladatelství Leges, Praha, 2016.

Králík, Michal: *Právo ve sportu (Law in sport)*, C.H. Beck, Praha, 2001.

Kubíček, Jiří: *Sport a právo (Sport and law)*, Masarykova univerzita, Brno, 2012.

Selected Bibliography

Raban, Přemysl: *Alternativní řešení sporů, arbitráž a rozhodci v České a Slovenské Republice a zahraničí (The Alternative dispute resolution, The Arbitration and Arbitrators in Czech and Slovak Republic and abroad)*, C. H. Beck, Praha, 2004.

Růžička, Květoslav: *Rozhodčí řízení před Rozhodčím soudem při Hospodářské komoře České republiky a Agrární komoře České republiky (The Arbitration Proceedings at the Arbitration Court attached to the Economic Chamber of Czech Republic and the Agricultural Chamber of the Czech Republic)*, Aleš Čeněk, Pelhřimov, 2003.

Various Authors: *Otázky sportovního práva (the Questions of Sports Law)*, Ústav státu a práva, Praha, 2008.

Various Authors: *Sportovní právo (Sports law)*, Auditorium, Praha, 2012.

Zoubek, Vladimír: *Postmoderní problémy lidských práv a globální bezpečnosti (Postmodern problems of human rights and global security)*, Aleš Čeněk, Plzeň, 2004.

Index

The numbers here refer to paragraph numbers

Made in the USA
Monee, IL
13 September 2026

62974283R00063